Long Blues
in A Minor

Long Blues
in A Minor

Gérard Herzhaft

Translated by John DuVal

The University of Arkansas Press
Fayetteville   London   *1988*

Originally published as *Un long blues en la mineur*,
© 1986 Editions Ramsay
Copyright © 1988 by Gérard Herzhaft
All rights reserved
Manufactured in the United States of America
92   91   90   89   88   5   4   3   2   1

Designer: Chiquita Babb
Typeface: Linotron 202 Trump Medieval
Typesetter: G&S Typesetters, Inc.
Printer: Thomson-Shore, Inc.
Binder: John H. Dekker & Sons, Inc.

The paper used in this publication meets the minimum
requirements of the American National Standard for
Permanence of Paper for Printed Library Materials
Z39.48-1984. ∞

Library of Congress Cataloging-in-Publication Data

Herzhaft, Gérard.
    [Long blues en la mineur. English]
    Long blues in A minor / Gérard Herzhaft : translated by
John DuVal.
    p. cm.
    Translation of: Un long blues en la mineur.
    ISBN 1-55728-036-3 (alk. paper).   ISBN 1-55728-037-1
(pbk. : alk. paper)
    I. Title.
    PQ2668.E725L613 1988   88-20504
    843'.914—dc19   CIP

To Juliette and to David.

They are tomorrow.

Long Blues
in A Minor

ONE

He was sitting down. Always sitting. Sitting and bent over. With a pair of tweezers in his hand and a monocle wedged into his right eye socket, he opened clock faces and poked into the little mechanisms. All around him lay gutted watches, alarm clocks that wouldn't go off, and chimes that wouldn't chime. He would toy with them for a long time, readjusting a screw with his tweezers, setting a new spring. Then the watches would keep time again, the alarms would go off again, and the chimes would chime. I rarely saw his face, even though it was bathed by the lamp that lit up the mechanisms he worked on. The glare must have strained his eyes after so many hours.

For me, he was a back more than anything else, bent forward under his oppressive, endless task. Sometimes he was also a grave voice saying "Clock repair is a clean trade."

For me, his back was a shadow, wide but fragile, heavy but elusive, nothing but a backbone arched over for checking and repairing time pieces, a human being's frail and crumbling spinal column.

One day during my bleak adolescence, on a twilit winter beach by a green sea under a gray sky, the black man loomed up before me.

I'm sure he had been watching me, but I hadn't seen him there, his dark form against the gathering night. I was throwing my knife at a broken boat hull cast ashore by the sea, an old carcass slimed over with seaweed and shells. A perfect target for my blade.

Suddenly there he stood in front of me. I felt a brief but real fear; this end of the beach was deserted and no one knew I was down here. I felt better when I saw his bare feet. I couldn't imagine someone attacking me in bare feet. Then somehow his big body, constrained by the familiar American uniform, his long, pleasant, smiling black face, his thick, crinkly hair, his cap threaded under the strap on his shoulder, his rolled up pantlegs revealing two huge feet and two giant big toes—everything said that this was a kind and easy-going man.

He spoke to me in clumsy French. "You're aiming better each time."

And he jerked the knife from the wood.

". . . but you need a real target. Look here!"

He pointed to an *O* that had once been part of the boat's name, painted in red and now half-erased by time and the sea, which sometimes washed up that far. He poised the knife, half shut his eyes, and threw. Suddenly the knife, my knife, stood right in the middle of the letter. I stared at it, wide eyed.

"Don't move!" he said.

He threw a large dagger from his belt. "You point, then you throw."

But he had already thrown, and the dagger was stuck in the wood a few millimeters from the knife, a big white blade that you wouldn't have thought could occupy so small a space, overshadowing what now looked like a little penknife, like me, I guess, a puny French teenager, next to him, a giant American GI.

I couldn't hold back a whistle of admiration, and I spoke to him for the first time, stammering something like, "*Ben, alors!*" or "*Dites donc!*" Whatever the interjection, it was a historic speech. It earned me a friendly pat on the head.

At that moment I felt that something important had happened in my life. And that's how it was that Sugar— William was his name, but everybody called him Sugar—came to be my friend that winter.

God knows the winter was cold, exceptionally harsh for those coasts along the English Channel where the weather was usually mild. The temperature stuck stubbornly below freezing. I shivered all the way to school, *supplementary school*, as they were calling it, a prefabricated hut typical of a lot of new post-war buildings.

The first-hour teacher had, in addition to his teaching duties, the formidable task of feeding the enormous stove in the corner by the blackboard. A coal bucket hung next to the stove, and it was our job—students in gray shirts, the uniform of the time, the season, the town, and my life—to keep the bucket full. All winter we filled and filled, and the teacher fed. For two classes of geometry, it smoked everywhere. We coughed through the class in ethics. And we filled and he fed. It got so cold icebergs appeared on the English Channel, something no fisherman had ever heard of before.

Still, that winter shone for me, because I had Sugar for a friend. He seemed to be attached to me, I never did know why. Whatever, he was a friend, my friend, American, black, huge, solid, loaded with chewing gum and chocolate. And cigarettes. (He gave me those, too, and I'd go off and smoke them in secret.) He was a

3

friend I could find on the frozen beach, in the bistro with the smell of french fries and mussels marinière, and in town, where I showed him the nooks and crannies, the dockyards and the rubble. Everything in town was either ruins or reconstruction. The city had been almost entirely destroyed except for one tiny medieval rampart and a few blocks of houses here and there. But already, the cranes were stirring, trucks were moving, crews of men were taking turns clearing away the stones, wood, and glass, throwing up scaffolds, and laying foundations for new buildings and a new city.

The town, which had always been active, with its fishermen coming in and going out day and night, had become a hive, teeming and humming, swollen with thousands of workers who were constantly busy, earning money and spending it. It was a great time for the few businesses that had survived the destruction and for the owners of the seedy cafes and taverns that had been thrown up for the workers. And for the Americans. After liberating us they were now confined close to their base outside town, but they were present everywhere, spreading the all-conquering Dollar everywhere as they strolled in groups along the half-destroyed or half-reconstructed streets. At night they drank, gambled, fought, and chased the girls, and the MPs roamed the town, harvesting GIs who had passed out drunk, foraging into dens of iniquity, routing out AWOLs or brawlers and carting them off to the military prison.

"Stay here! Keep a look out!" Sugar would tell me, depositing me at the counter of the Brasserie du Port with beers, french fries, and lots of coins for the pinball machines that America had brought along with its armies. Then Sugar would sit off in a corner with some delightful young thing, usually Thérèse, whose light-blonde hair flooded her carefully madeup face. He would be drinking, laughing, whispering something to

4

her in his irresistible franglais. Then, invariably after twenty minutes (I would time them on my watch), they would rise together and climb the stairs to the second floor, toward other heavens. And I would go on drinking, eating, and playing the machine. The coins would jingle into the slot and the machine would light up along the path of the metal ball, which I guided more and more skillfully with each visit to the Brasserie du Port. I twisted my legs in front of the pinball machine and with my fingers I caressed it, cajoled it, shook it, struck it, and the pretty blonde *Americaine*— Sue, Cynthia, Tina, maybe even Thérèse—yielded finally to my assaults, lit up and gave me a free game.

"Stay here! Keep a look out!" And I would stay there and look out with my eye on the door and my ear cocked toward the street, drinking, playing, and watching for the redoubtable MP jeep in the night. I never let Sugar down and the two times the military police did come to rout out late GIs, I beat them to it. A quick rap at the door, and Sugar was surging up like a devil and running toward the back door, flinging on his shirt and jumping into his pants as he ran, yelling *"Thanks, boy!"* in English, a thanks that made up for the long evening's waiting and would ring in my ears through the long days that followed, a manly, affectionate pat on the head from my good friend Sugar.

And so the year went by as I ran from school to my family's house to the base, but more and more from school straight to the base. I lived by Sugar's schedule and kept company with soldiers, who no longer killed anything except the time that separated them from their return home and reunion with their loved ones on American soil.

As a sergeant, Sugar shared his small room with only one other man, Mack, another black sergeant. The chief occupations of these two, while they were in their room, seemed to be drinking wine and playing poker. The wine they ordered through me, and I procured it as fast as I could. As they played poker, I browsed wonderingly through their voluminous library of dog-eared and sometimes torn comic books. The text was often difficult, but that only added to the mystery of the adventures and my fascination with the strange heroes I was discovering. This was before they captivated the rest of the world. The masked heroes fascinated me most: what were those strange beings hidden behind scraps of cloth? Behind the eye holes the illustrators had painted nothing. There was the Lone Ranger, or *Justicier Solitaire* as I translated, with his silver bullets, his pure white horse, and his Indian friend Tonto who followed him, stood by him, and always and everywhere rescued him. And the Phantom, whose powerful pectoral muscles swelled his gym suit, whose head was wrapped in a kind of ski helmet, and whose black mask also revealed no human eye behind it: The Ghost who Walks! And Drago, Zorro, Amok, and so many others. And Sugar?—who would, maybe, some day take off his black mask and appear as he really was, to me, his friend. The Lone Ranger and Tonto!

The immediate consequence of my friendship with Sugar and his friends was a plummeting in my grades at school. But at the same time, I was gaining a firmer grip on the American language and on the vivid, colorful, flexible, striking black slang, something that would eventually be very useful.

As they gambled and drank in their room, Mack and Sugar listened to a strange, discordant music that didn't resemble at all the music my family listened to—nothing like Patrice or Mario, Rina Ketty or Luis Mariano. These were blacks, singing in black American for black GIs. Sometimes a trumpet or a saxophone would strike a familiar note, recalling Ray Ventura or Jacques Helian, who made our Saturday dances so pleasant. But usually it was just one singer alone with extraordinary instrumental sounds that I learned only later to identify, but which now seemed like a solid block of noise: terribly heavy electric guitars, harmonicas so amplified that they sounded like brasses, and thick drawling voices. It was all disharmonious to me, and one record never seemed to vary from the next. Many was the time during the long hours I spent leafing through comic books in their room that I would heave a sigh of relief when one of the 78's reached the end of its turns. But the respite was brief. Invariably, one of the sergeants would put a record back on. The same one or the other side, it was all the same to me.

One day Mack and Sugar were drinking and listening and nodding their heads to a song. Suddenly, although nothing remarkable had happened that I could see, Mack broke down sobbing. His friend offered him a glass and said, "Here, drink it. It helps you forget."

And the singer finished:

And she said, Man, I don't want you no more, get back overseas.

I couldn't understand the whole meaning, but I did understand that this music from across the world which moved them so much was part of Sugar's universe, as much as the card games, the pin-ups on the wall, the Lone Ranger, and the Phantom.

So I started little by little trying to decipher the labels that circled the holes in the middle of the records. Columbia had its musical notes, Bluebird its blue bird on a yellow background, Chess its horse head. They were soon familiar symbols. One day, when he had seen that I was interested, Sugar gave me a stack of records: "Here, take 'em!"

7

He had often given me comics and cigarettes and even small change as a way of thanking me for the little errands I ran for him, so at the time I didn't think much of these new gifts. The records were obviously worn, and besides, the record player at home was for the exclusive use of my father. So I contented myself with stacking the wax discs up in a neat pile next to the comics, which I leafed through night after night. Once in a while, between my favorite masked heroes and a Tarzan adventure, I would pick them up and look at the logos, which seemed to be dancing around the center: the laughing Columbia notes, the elegant Bluebird, and the stern Chess knight. Then I would put them neatly away. They still weren't music for me, anyway. They were symbols of a strange world, the exotic, benevolent world of Sugar. Often as I fell asleep, the Chess knight galloped over hurdles of black notes—black like the face of my friend—and they would jump and dance, observed by the imperturbable eye of the bird as it stretched its blue wings.

Then one day the inevitable happened, though I had never wanted to admit it would. It was a beautiful day in June with a cool breeze pushing little waves onto the shore, as I headed for the base carrying two bottles of red wine.

When I reached the barracks room, everything was topsy-turvy, closets open, shelves empty, stuff piled on the beds. No one was there, but I could hear snatches of conversation and bursts of laughter from the room next door. Not knowing what to do, I stood for a moment with a bottle hanging from each hand, trying to listen in on the voices and make some sense out of the disorder around me. Finally I walked toward where the sounds were coming from. The room was full of sergeants and other enlisted men, some whites and lots of blacks, standing around with glasses in their hands, celebrating something.

The forest of uniforms was shaking with laughter and conviviality. I couldn't help spotting Sugar's fuzzy head above the others. A long moment passed, him in the middle of his own people, beige and black, drinking, laughing, talking; me, screwed down to the doorway, in my shabby school uniform, with a bottle in each hand to keep me balanced. Then his face turned toward me, and his eyes, sympathetic and kind, met mine. With a wink he invited me over. He slapped me on the back as I held the bottles out to him.

"Thanks, boy, thanks!" and he went on in his broken French: "*Mack et moi, on part.* Go back to America."

A meteorite struck me, but he went on, excited, joyful. "This is it. This time *la guerre* really is *finie!* Boat leaves tomorrow. Destination New York. Then on to Chicago!"

He drank a big draught from his glass.

"This is it, boy, this is it. Back home! Back home!"

Hemmed in by the crowd of grown-ups, jostled this way and that, I didn't think. I was glad for Sugar's joy, but I was sad, so sad, at losing him.

A little later, in his room, he said his goodbyes.

"So long, boy. So long."

I didn't really listen as he told me, more and more in English, about all he was going to do when he got back to his own country, about his family who had been waiting for him all those years, his girl friend who maybe hadn't waited for him, his little house somewhere down South where his mother still lived, his brother lying in a small corner of Norman sand, who wouldn't be going "back home" with him. I just heard his strong, comforting voice, saw his face, his giant's

9

body, his big-brother hands, his indulgent-daddy manners, and I realized how much I loved that great black man who for one winter had been my pal, my friend, my father, my guide, one I had probably been waiting for without knowing it.

Sugar could sense my sorrow but he couldn't hide his own joy or find the right words to tell me goodbye. He stuffed a big gunny sack with comics and records and handed it to me. "These are yours, boy. So you'll remember the good old times."

Though he usually stayed in his room when I left, this time he walked me down to my bicycle. And as I pressed down on the pedal to start off, with the big canvas sack crammed full of America swaying precariously on my bicycle basket, he walked a little ways beside me:

"Say goodbye to Thérèse for me."

There was a long, vast silence, and he added, "*Au revoir*, old man. Don't be sad. We'll be seeing each other again."

As I started out through the main gate, he clapped me so hard on the shoulders I almost lost my balance.

"See you in Chicago! *A bientôt!*" he shouted. And he trotted back toward his room.

Au revoir, Sugar, *au revoir!* I'll be all alone without you this summer and next winter! And maybe all the winters after.

I was lonely as I pedaled past the docks, threaded my way through lines of cranes and scaffolding, and bounced and bumped over the patched-up streets, weighed down by a great canvas sack where the Phantom collided with Superman, and Mandrake danced with Flash Gordon to the records, while the blue bird, the black knight, and the Columbia notes struggled together to watch over the world. The land of Sugar in a sack, America triumphant, mysterious, exotic, fascinating. The black soldier's America. Sugar's America.

The next day, I climbed up to the Calvaire du Marin, an anonymous cross perched on a hill overlooking the port, hoping to be in on the military departure from a distance. I thought I could see, among the embarking troops, the tall silhouette of my friend, still straight even under the weight of his duffle bag.

Above the noises of the port—the ships and the boats, the trucks and jeeps roaring about, the sea and the seagulls—I thought I could hear Sugar's voice. It was an illusion, I know, but I couldn't help calling back:

"*Au revoir*, Sugar, *à bientôt*. See you in Chicago!"

TWO

A few years passed, full of fumblings, failures, successes. The winter without Sugar, which the spring had forecast would be so bleak, passed without any real problem. Summer weather had swept Sugar away. Or at least that's what I thought. But to the astonishment of my teachers, I began to apply myself more and more to learning English, made rapid progress, and soon became the star pupil in the subject.

Little by little adolescence gave way to adulthood, and as I came to understand the words inside the bubbles better—often just a series of onomatopoetic phrases or sentence fragments—Sugar's comic books lost their appeal. Even the masked heroes became one-dimensional and predictable, lost their mystery, and bored me. Only the masks themselves, eyeless and hiding a strange, unfathomable void, held their fascination. The comics burrowed deeper into their corner in the closet, under other books, diaries, school notebooks, like layers under geological layers.

During my teenage years, I never listened to Sugar's

records. By the time I had my own record player, the old 78's had been replaced by long-playing records in bright jackets. But my taste in music was American. I listened to Cochran, Elvis, and Lonnie Donegan, an odd Scotsman with a face like a letter opener and a voice like a police siren, who adapted and reworked American folk themes. I knew that behind their music lay the world of Sugar.

Sugar's records had joined his comics in the sterile void of tears never shed and goodbyes at the dock, buried, but always there, sustained notes that could only be measured by other sorrows and other hurts.

My little town on the English Channel had been rebuilt of concrete blocks, and I was getting ready to leave it for greener and vaster pastures where I could go on studying the language of Shakespeare and Sugar. Sorting through my belongings as I got ready to leave, I happened on that old stack of 78 records. I hesitated a second before putting them back, perhaps forever, into the depths of the closet, but as I took a last quick look the logos came to life again, the black knight, the Columbia notes, the blue bird. The year of Sugar rushed brutally back into my mind, the strolls along the docks, the Brasserie du Port, the American base, the barracks room, and for an instant good old Sugar loomed up behind me and slapped me on the back. One second of hesitation, but that was all, and the old records slid into my suitcase, sandwiched between a blue sweater and some underwear.

It would take some time before I got around to listening to them—and a lot of luck and a second-hand record player that could play 78's. That's how life is: a series of chance events pushing you in one direction toward an overwhelming discovery which, sure, something inside you has also aimed for, but which, even so, without that little shove of chance, you could never have reached. That's probably how Christopher Columbus discovered America. Anyway, that's how I discovered mine, the America of the blues.

I remember that day as if it were yesterday. The smallest details are engraved in my mind: my little attic room, the bed and a few chairs, the desk piled with books and scribbled notes, how tired I was after a long day of studying by myself. And the rain pattering on the fanlight. And rock records, too (they were beginning to lose their appeal . . . , they lacked something, something I hadn't managed to define yet, but something basic). I remember looking for some not-too-intellectual book to relax with. Rummaging deeper into my stuff, I dug up the records Sugar had given me.

Amused and a little nostalgic, I examined the logos again, and again the old memories came back. Then, probably for the first time, I read the titles and the names of the artists. It was like my first meeting with Sugar, one look discovering a new world. Even the names of the musicians were poems: Howlin' Wolf, Muddy Waters, Leadbelly. I read them aloud in English, and then again in French: *le Loup Hurlant, les Eaux Boueuses, Ventre de Plomb!* And then the titles, which sounded familiar because of similar titles on my rock records: "Milk Cow Blues" and "Rolling Stone," which a young English rock group would later adopt as its own name and make famous.

I spent that night listening to those records. I had never really heard them before. Beneath the scratches, which the needle transmitted with the highest fidelity, the twisted guitars, the racing pianos, the mournful harmonicas, and most of all those extraordinary deep voices, heavy with life and with despair, revealed to me little by little a mysterious world, near and yet far away, another planet beneath my feet, in my head and in my heart. As the days passed, the old records turned more and more under the needle. This was the music that had made Sugar and Mack laugh or cry. And I realized that this was the rock music I was used to, with something added, a human, moving, spellbinding soul, a whirlwind of powerful, evocative images. One of the singers was always running from an omnipresent danger personified as *the hounds of Hell.* Another wanted to be reincarnated as a catfish, because *all the pretty women want to fish for him.* A third was a little red rooster that crowed to warn all the neighbors to *keep an eye on their wives and their daughters.* The same singer, this time *the man that comes in the back door,* explained that *the men don't know me, but the women know me well.* The one I came to like best was Big Johnny White. He had a deep, rich voice that martyred the speaker and rose above the crackling of the grooves. These were records Sugar and Mack had played and over-played. Big Johnny White! Usually it was just him and a guitar—electric or electrified, it was hard to tell—, sometimes with a drummer, a steam engine beating joyfully along. Fairly often there was also an amazing sound I couldn't identify at the time but which I learned later was a metal tube scraped along the strings.

She is my sweet little angel Big Johnny muttered, and his guitar would keep going, on up to paradise, airy, velvety. Wonderful.

Big Johnny White! I listened and relistened to that mysterious, compelling stranger as attentively as I had listened ten years earlier to Sugar. Slowly but irresistibly that music became an important part of my life. I started looking for blues albums at the record shops, but they were hard to find. Blues music was still unknown in France, and even the music store owners got blues mixed up with jazz.

I also started putting in hours of intense guitar practice. I had begun playing a few years before, but hadn't made much real progress. I could twang out a few chords to accompany my Lonnie Donegan records, but my repertoire was extremely limited. With Big Johnny White, all that changed. Just as once with Sugar I had worked at a fantastic dialogue that initiated me into a world totally unlike the one around me, I now formed a different kind of relationship with Big Johnny. Underneath the jolting of the needle, he would sing and play his guitar, sweet and angry, calm and violent, tender and tough, trembling to the whim of the old record's surface, and I would follow him the way I had followed Sugar, pupil to master. But this was an unwilling master, imprisoned in wax. A strict pupil, I held him to the task and made him do the lesson over and over a hundred times without letup, chord to chord, note to note, guitar to guitar, blues to blues.

Imperceptibly, day after day, night after night, Big Johnny delivered up his secrets to my fingers as they wore and hardened on the metal strings. And what secrets! Extravagant chords that allowed for effects never heard before, trembling vibratos, angelic glissades, cascades of notes, accompanying, underlining, clothing the voice of the singer. That was a new year of America. Once more a black man from over there was in my life, this time contained in magic little wax discs whose musical hieroglyphics were mine to decipher. And I was Champollion. I learned Big Johnny's world, I played his music, I took possession of his guitar, I shared his blues.

My guitar became my inseparable companion: beautiful, blonde, with harmonious curves and sensitive strings that I stroked to make her laugh or weep or moan. I played like Big Johnny. I sang like Big Johnny. Was I Big Johnny? As a matter of fact, who *was* Big Johnny White? An American; okay. A black man, sure. But how old? What did he look like? Where did he hang out? Chicago? Detroit? Mississippi? Was he still alive? The map of the United States, which I already knew by heart from having searched it through and through for the ghost of Sugar, took on new interest. Big Johnny White, old man, I wanted to know you where you lived, put a shape and a face on your name, a mouth around your voice, hands on your guitar, eyes on your blues.

I started playing in public, here and there, in the streets or in cafes. But the times weren't yet ready for that music. Street singers all sounded like Mouloudji and René-Louis Lafforgue:

"*D'ou viens-tu, gitan? Je viens de Bohême.*"

And I would echo in American:

Gonna' get up tomorrow mornin', gonna shake out my mop.
Gonna' get up tomorrow mornin', gonna shake out my mop.
My baby left me yesterday. Anyone can have my job.

At that time playing the guitar in the streets wasn't considered altogether proper, and there were risks. The police would swoop down without warning, and pow! rough up this menace to public tranquillity: what are you trying to do with that guitar? Smother the squeals of the tires? Muffle the exhaust pipes? Drown out the horns? What a sorry example you're setting for little kids, singing that stuff in the streets! That's not even music, Monsieur! That jungle noise? We aren't Negroes here, Monsieur! Besides, why play the guitar at all, when we have the television? Let other people do the singing. Isn't that better than disturbing the peace?

One, then another, guitar delicately smashed by the defenders of law and order in the line of duty, a few hard slaps in the face, and one last punch, applied with a little more force than the others to the pit of the stomach, earning me a few weeks of difficult breathing, were enough to cut short my budding vocation. I got the message. I sheathed my guitar, swallowed my blues, and didn't sing in the streets anymore. You can rest easy, Big Johnny White.

But the records kept turning, getting worn out from use, wearing out my needles, too, but soothing my ears and sharpening my mind as I explored unknown worlds. Here was a music of suffering and fierce pride, and it struck a chord deep inside me, a human and sensual chord. The guitars and voices danced with each other, answered and caressed each other, clawing the air and battering my heart. What is music, anyway, that it can move us so? And who was I to be responding with such fire to an unknown black man?

More than ever America was a blues horizon I looked toward. My musical career, interrupted on the public streets by the agents of order and the mood of the times, continued in private, more intensely than ever. And my dialogue with voices and fingers across the sea continued, became more serious and somber, and began to weigh on my spirits. But when my studies at the university ended and my small scholarship was gone, I had to go out and look for work.

After a few false starts, a few jobs that fortunately didn't pan out, a few doors shut in my face, I landed a position in a prestigious civil service sector responsible for correspondence with the Anglo-Saxon world.

Public Administration was a new shock for me. I don't know what I expected to find when I went into it—a sense of service, active work, a certain security. My nose had warned me that not all the rumors about administrative ineptitude could be wrong, and I quickly learned that the reality outdid the rumor. *Travail assis*, work sitting down, is what they called desk work, and that's what it was. The measly correspondence they consented to turn over to me had first been filtered, prepared, and checked by an assistant supervisor of questionable linguistic competence, and then enumerated, annotated and paperclipped by a supervisor in his big private office, who morning, noon, and night kept himself informed, nitpicking, questioning, scrutinizing, checking and rechecking to make sure that none of his colleagues made themselves too important and, above all, that none of them cast a doubt on his own importance. Starting at eight in the morning, a pool of nice, chattery typists attended to their business: recipes and diapers for the married ones, flirtations and other adventure for the singles, detailed commentaries on last night's TV shows for all. The spiked heels, lipstick, skirt lengths, bust sizes, and real or imagined favors from the supervisors and assistant supervisors were material for hundreds of dime-novels.

Plots tangled and untangled: these against those, those against others. Hastily-contrived alliances ended with shattering betrayals. Any two people would refuse to speak to each other; then suddenly they were sharing their most intimate secrets again. They would chatter on and on for hours, on the corners of the desks, around the typewriters, against the Coke machines. They were friends and would swear eternal friendship. But the next day a makeup that was too garish or a friendly word from the supervisor, and one of them would end up pouting. Sweetly cruel comments would lash their dollfaces, and tears would furrow their foundation cream. Installed in one corner, too young, too humble, and too without-rank to arouse the least passion or interest in these married or unmarried ladies, I translated away at the few papers allotted me.

"You got here just in time!" the assistant supervisor had said as she rubber-stamped a stack of papers, "We're already six months behind."

So I threw myself, heart and body, into the task of closing the gap, and in forty-eight hours it was closed. From the looks the assistant supervisor gave me and the frowns of the supervisor, I realized the enormity of my error. I had broken the cadence and discredited the refrain: "We're overworked," "We're understaffed," "The working conditions must be improved!" For ages the supervisor had been paperclipping, the assistant supervisor had been stamping, the typists had been typing (careful not to damage their fingernails), and the work had stopped up, the forms had stacked up, the deadlines had passed, until the eventful and inevitable moment when a supplementary position had to be created. This reassuring liturgy might have gone on till the end of bureaucratic time, but here came a certain young upstart and with one blow—you know how it is with kids these days if they've had a little college—knocked all the idols down, stepped up the music, and kicked over the red-tape Paternoster.

"Ah! But things aren't done like that! This kid is going to learn what's what!"

The whole system of checks and control went into high gear. All letters were viewed and reviewed before being transmitted to me. Then I had to transmit mine to the Assistant Supervisor, who, with infinite precautions, would read, re-read and paperclip them before transmitting them to the Supervisor's desk, where they would lie gathering dust until they were finally sent. Often close inspection would finally reveal a word or figure of speech that failed to please, and the Supervisor would call in the Assistant Supervisor, who would hand the shameful page back to me with a caustic, "Too much haste, and we make mistakes!"

I've never been much of a revolutionary. As quickly as the police had taught me not to compete with Big Johnny White on French territory, the Supervisor and Assistant Supervisor now converted me to their concept of administrative duty. I adopted the lowest profile possible and took my example from them: I let the letters pile up, I constructed a joyous disorder upon my desk, and in all circumstances I conserved a grave and thoughtful attitude in keeping with the capital importance of the mission entrusted to me by France. And in the midst of a chaos of correspondence, I found time to read a book, decipher some lines of music, and catch up on my personal letter writing.

After that, no more snide remarks and insinuations, no more letters returned to do over. I had found the correct pitch and measure required of my small part in the Grand Administrative Orchestra. My supervisors soon forgot me, and for a while I got along in peace, living off the State, and the State required nothing of me except that I keep my mouth shut. But sometimes it was hard to concentrate on de Maupassant's prose, Count Basie's notations, or the weekly letter home. The giggles and clucks of my colleagues, their tears and their screams, the constant comings and goings from the desks to the bathrooms to the coffee machine (the office obstacle course, run a hundred times a day) disturbed my concentration and confused my thoughts, and I found my attention more and more riveted to the clock, which at long last pointed to deliverance at five o'clock and sent me hurtling out of the office. If only the Walkman had been invented then! I could have passed the whole day with my blues-singer friends to the satisfaction of the Supervisor, the Assistant Supervisor, and my colleagues.

But I shouldn't be unjust. These women were very nice, very sweet, very pleasant to look at, and their perfumes smelled good. Their bustling and rustling added welcome feminity to that cramped, gray bureaucratic world. From time to time they sat at their typewriters and typed, allowing me to concentrate on my novel.

At widely spaced but regular intervals life in the Service was interrupted by the announced or sometimes even unannounced appearance of the Great Supervisor, the Supervisor-in-Chief, who would condescend to descend one floor to see how the Office was getting on. He was a good old boy, grown gray in the service, who himself had once been an Assistant Supervisor, and then a Supervisor, before becoming what he was, so he knew that one must not disturb the Administrative Liturgy. He belched up a few incomprehensible syllables, probably meant as encouragement for my colleagues in skirts and me in our production of red tape, listened gravely to the Assistant Supervisor's incongruent and unworkable suggestions, (intended to win her, at last, perhaps, her long-desired promotion), and then closed himself up for some time with the Supervisor in the Supervisor's office. The typewriters crackled, bladders that usually filled up early went unemptied till noon, throats usually parched went without water, and the coffee machine went unplugged, for once relieved of spitting out its little cups and pouring out its dubious black liquid. Such an unendurable tension could not last. The Supervisor-in-Chief came out of the Supervisor's office, taking his leave with a kind word: "Please convey my satisfaction to your people."

Or more likely: "I'll consider your request for additional personnel."

And he would leave our world, nodding his head toward us with a faint smile.

A few more humdrum months of this lulled me into a cottony calm I might have smothered in if the blues hadn't pulled me out. I had divided my life between my work at the Administration and the music I listened to and played more and more. And I was still searching desperately for more blues records. At the flea market, in bins marked "Jazz" by sellers who didn't know a thing about the blues, I found plenty to feed my passion: lots of old 78's and some new LPs, obtained partly from enlightened collectors, but mostly from black GIs on their way home. My collection grew rapidly, as did my familiarity with themes and instrumental figures, but the faces of the artists remained as blank as ever.

By now I had dozens of Big Johnny White records, mostly in 78's, but a few 45's, too, a good sign that my involuntary tutor and initiator-in-chief to the blues was still alive and cutting records. He was singing and playing the guitar and this time he was accompanied by an extraordinarily good harmonica player, pouring out wave after chromatic wave. The song was "Highway 49."

I was doing all right with you, baby, but I had to move on.
I was doing all right with you, baby, but I had to move on.
When the rooster crowed this morning, I was on High-
     way 49.

The next morning, by the time the alarm went off, I had made up my mind to quit my job.

I announced my decision as soon as I got to work.

23

This plunged the Assistant Supervisor into a well of perplexity.

"You realize you're in line for a promotion?" she confided to me in a murmur of reproach.

"Right," I answered, "that's why it's time to quit."

Consternation and hurt registered on her crinkled face. Her thick eyebrows rose in question marks above her curved beak. My announcement was revolutionary for these regions, and it opened immeasurable gulfs of uncertainty beneath her.

"But . . . your career?" she gasped. Whole partitions of her life were crumbling: evaluations, promotions, sliding pay scales on locked-in positions, career advancements, immutable schedules tumbled one upon the other, as it dawned on her that I was saying that none of those things interested me. Usually distant and formal, she was now feverish and agitated, and she grasped my wrist, pleading for reassurance: "You've passed another exam. You're going into another administration. You've found a position in a higher slot!"

"No, no!" I tried to tell her. "All I want is to play my guitar and listen to music. The office weighs me down. I'm suffocating. I'm dying of it. I need a little air!"

But she kept on, feverish, squeezing me into a corner, lowering her voice so that I could confide, intimately, the real reason for my departure. "He doesn't want to announce it out loud for all the secretaries to hear," she was probably telling herself, "but to me, his hierarchical superior, he may confess. He will tell me. He will tell me! I must have the answer!"

The creases in her brow and her livid complexion gave her face the look of elegant letterhead paper. I took pity on her at last and confided in a whisper, "Yes, I've secured a position in another ministry, in a slightly better grade."

I spent a few weeks living my life to the rhythm of

the blues: records, guitar, flea market. The meager savings shored up during my administrative job were slipping away. The Running-out-of-Money Blues didn't much appeal to me. Steaks for dinner gave way to hard boiled eggs, and I still had to pay the rent. When I didn't even have money to replace the guitar strings that I had strummed, stroked and plucked to a frazzle, I was forced to face the fact that I had to find work. So once again, the Job-search Saraband: newspapers read at dawn, as soon as they came out, spread open to the want ads on greasy cafe counters and marked with a red pencil; early morning workers' laughter and their shouts to each other; the smell of coffee steaming; a croissant melting sweetly in my mouth and crumbling on the printed page. Then the telephone calls, the knocking at doors, the polite refusals, the impolite rebuffs, the interminable waits; the drawn faces of other applicants, the look in their eyes from the days, weeks, months maybe, gone by with no result. A job! Any job! It was a poor little world of applicants, with deflated tomorrows, bills to pay, children to feed.

One thing I can tell you, sang Eddie Boyd on one of my records, *the blues are here to stay.*

At least all I had to feed was my guitar.

Some half-hearted applications, some doors shut in my face, an import-export house that worked at a Stakhanovite rhythm I couldn't keep up with, and once again I landed an administrative post. But not just any administration this time: the great, the only! The National Library hired me to handle the collections of English and American periodicals it received in exchange for French ones. This was, *a priori* I felt, the perfect position for me. For me, the library was still a place of peace, calm, and meditation, a place set aside for culture, where I had long before discovered *Tintin, The Viscount of Bragelonne, The Hunchback of Notre*

Dame, The Count of Monte-Cristo. And as a university student, I had gone there to get warm; to get to know another student, hard at work on her books; or to doze between classes, propped up against the copying machine and chewing on a caramel from the handy machine at the entrance. And so at first the National Library conformed to my expectations: humdrum dominated.

White-haired scholars, bent under the weight of their years and knowledge, waited in long lines for the precious book of spells, the original leather-bound text, or an issue of a journal long since out of circulation. A team of shelvers in gray shirts and sad faces came and went among the tall stacks, shelving and unshelving, taking books back and giving them out again. Others on the staff checked the identity of all who entered. Each researcher, scholar, or professor had to produce a reference card, stamped and initialed with a photograph clipped on, conferring admittance to those sacred precincts. Everywhere a velvety silence reigned, and a vague, sweetish odor of dust and mildew wreathed upward along the tall columns and steel beams toward a high unwashed stained-glass window that flooded the vast hall with glaucous light, calling to mind the railroad stations of the Second Empire; only this station was without trains or tracks, where the travelers stayed put, forever reading in a vast waiting room, hunched over school desks.

The librarians responsible for "animating" the holdings were titled *conservateurs*, or should I say *conservatrices*, because they were so predominantly feminine, although this particular genre of femininity I had never come upon before, and it was hard to place it in the cycle of human evolution: there were few married women and hardly any young single women. Their gray hair was drawn back into tight buns. Their faces were lean, shriveled, and parchment-dry, but you could not read any emotion on them. Their figures, too, were indecipherable under colorless, shapeless dresses. They pit-patted endlessly among the manuscripts, jealously keeping watch. They seemed strange creatures from another world whose existence people on the outside didn't even suspect, fierce guardians over knowledge they did not care to share, vestals of a temple of yellowed papers and leather bindings, bibliotechnocrats whose age could not be determined except perhaps with carbon 14. . . .

There were a few exceptions, however, way out of tune with the rest: agents under contract, specialists in one area or one language, refugees. There was that old Korean professor who had left everything to get away from a reign of absolute terror; his skin continued to yellow over the ancient manuscripts composed in the language of his ancestors, one whose secrets he alone could unlock. There was the middle-aged Czech lady whose iridescent dresses brightened the space around her, whose delicious accent formed r's deep in her throat, whose great blue eyes showed the trials she had suffered. All by herself she was the blues of Central Europe. If I could have introduced her to Big Johnny White, they would have understood each other.

This whole astonishing world could be found at the Library Canteen between noon and two o'clock every day. But the hierarchical divisions stayed in place. The shelvers, who had grayed under the stained-glass window, stuffed themselves with pastries dripping grease and exchanged inside information on the horseraces. The office workers made themselves a band apart and, just as elsewhere, dug around themselves an unbridgeable moat of recipes and baby words. The librarians, too, with sweeping signals to one another, reserved their tables, which they claimed with quick, small steps, balancing trays of lean food—raw vegetables, yogurt, and fruit. Through all these maneuvers, their chatter went on. These strange women, seemingly so detached from the material world, lived their lives to the rhythm of petty intrigues, intolerance, backbiting, belittling, calculated cruelties, and military hierarchies. Washed-out eyes would flame, diners would brandish forks, passionate inter-service quarrels would erupt: Manuscripts against Prints, Stamps against Prizes, Periodicals against them all.

Then back to work: manuscripts to guard, old books to watch over for mildew or the least trace of a death-watch beetle, thousands of new books to harvest, number, catalogue, rebind, and cram tighter into the olive-drab metal shelves, where they waited for the dust to settle on their edges. Then all would be well; henceforth, they belonged to the National Library.

A few months of this diet put a dent in my health, which until then had been fine. I started getting hollows around my eyes. I lost my appetite. My dreams started teeming with weird ghosts in lackluster, off-white sheets, the kind washed with brand X. Winter evenings when I got off work, twilight had already settled, which was just as well, because by now even the streetlights hurt my eyes, the neon lights assaulted me, and the stoplights had become intolerable bursts of red. I was losing my sense of taste and smell, lust and desire. Little by little, the National Library was taking possession of me.

One morning as I was shaving, a dull, yellowish film glared out at me. My face was drawn and pale, my hair lifeless. I was getting gray, soft, and parchment-dry, like the librarians around me. My skin was taking on the color of the shelvers. My heart was beating to the rhythm of "Please Be Quiet." Help, help! I was drowning in a bottomless pit of bookrooms and bookshelves, deluged by old bindings and mold. I was also turning to dust.

Even my records and guitar couldn't stir warmth back into my life. This time the sticky blues were getting under my skin.

One evening I came home the long way on foot, airing myself out and shaking off the National Library molecules. Walking fast, I crossed the Palais-Royal, passed the Samaritaine department store, and crossed the Seine without seeing it, although glad to feel its cold air slapping my face. Suddenly, somewhere in the Latin Quarter, a little bill tacked on a wall caught my notice. I had passed it without really seeing it, just a fleeting image I might have forgotten instantly, but something about it pulled me back to look again, more carefully. Surprise gave way to joy. It was just a little piece of paper, which read, *"MERCREDI, à 20 h 30, AUX TROIS MARTEAUX, LE GRAND BLUESMAN PIANO SLIM."* Piano Slim. I owned an excellent record of his that Sugar had given me when he left France. Piano Slim, who rolled out boogie-woogies as easily as rolling cigarettes. Piano Slim, with a creamy, rich voice that rose from a cloud of smoke and a keg of whiskey. Piano Slim, a bluesman, at last! Alive, in flesh and blood, here in Paris! I could hardly believe it! That set me right again, and it fired me up. I could barely wait till Wednesday evening.

I was one of the first to take a seat near the bar, in reach of the little stage the piano sat on. The Trois Marteaux was one of those dives typical of the Latin Quarter back then, where aging jazz lovers got together to jam, socialize, drink some wine, and listen.

Well-dressed, just ruffled enough to show they had

been out in the wind, with their shoes shined and *Le Monde* under their arms, they drifted in and sat down.

The jazz set had been avant-garde before the war, but they had not aged well. They had broken off into multiple clans, excommunicating one another and addressing proclamations at one another in reviews that had shrunk to hermetic bulletins, written in some Pharasaian, Parisian dialect proclaiming anathemas against this or that musician. As the ranks thinned, they had bade deserters good riddance. Then they had huddled more closely around the leaders of their Schools, or Classrooms, I should say, where half the seats were soon empty. Their leaders were popes, handing down revelations from on high: what to think, what to listen to, what to like. Revelations rained down, categorical, without appeal. Dizzy was not Jazz. On the other hand, Charlie *had* been, until that blunder of 1945, when he had done bop! And the herd shook their heads and drank in the words.

That Wednesday night, the room was full. People glared at each other between tables, and sneers and knowing snickers echoed back and forth. But the blues brought them together. Not that these jazz lovers understood the blues. Or that they liked it much. But it had been decreed that blues was the ancestor of jazz, and loving the child, they had come to pay respects to the grandfather.

And what a grandfather that evening! Piano Slim rose out of nowhere, a bulldozer, crushing the carpet with each huge step, hilarious and already reeling from alcohol. Slim? He might have been once, but he was a colossus today. He was in his early sixties, with a spot of white in his black hair. He sat down, muttered some words nobody understood, and started playing. The Blues. The same blues I had been listening to for so many years, but rising now from that piano right in

30

front of me, brought suddenly to life by the miracle of those long, tortured fingers, striking the keys with amazing speed.

I looked at Piano Slim and I saw Sugar. Maybe the concert wasn't all that good, I don't know, but that didn't matter to me. I was seeing a bluesman in action. Imagine a Latin scholar, living among his texts and the manuscripts of Caesar and Ammianus Marcellinus, seeing a citizen of ancient Rome suddenly walk into his life. But the more I listened to Piano Slim and watched him play and sing, the more I realized that his world was still living, on the other side of the Atlantic, an airplane flight away! The music I had steeped myself in for years, the culture I had guessed at, existed on my planet and in my era. The Latinist could go to Rome, but there he would find only ruins and frail shadows. I could live in that other world which had become half my life—go see it, touch it and hear it.

After the concert, Piano Slim and I had a talk. The others hemmed and hawed some awkward English out of Carpentier and Fialip's *Manuel d'Anglais Pratique*, which Piano Slim obviously couldn't understand a word of. But I spoke in Sugar's accent, with words I had learned from my blues records. We stayed a while, talking and drinking a few glasses at one of the tables until the manager was ready to take Slim back to his hotel. It was late, and I didn't want to impose on him any longer.

"Yeah," he told me, "in Chicago, you can hear lots of good blues."

And then, giving in to my mania, I asked him about some of the names I had learned from my records.

He answered, trying to locate each of them. "Sonny Boy? He's dead. Somebody murdered him in an alley. Muddy Waters? Yeah, I know him. We're good friends. He's a good man."

"And Big Johnny White?" I dared to ask.

"Him, he's a tough guy. He's here, there—you never can tell where he'll show up." He downed his whiskey. "Big Johnny, he goes back a long way. They don't make 'em like that anymore."

A little later, standing outside on the sidewalk, shivering, I watched his car pull away. He rolled down the window. "So long!," he yelled out. "See you in Chicago!"

The same words Sugar had shouted years ago. But then the separation had seemed impossible to bridge. Now I realized, yes, *sure*, how could I have been so dumb? I *could* see him in Chicago. All I had to do was get a passport and a visa. No time machine, no intergalactic rocket necessary. Just a simple airline ticket.

After that, the dust of the National Library weighed lighter on me. I didn't notice the hair buns or the gray shirts or the shapeless dresses. With my eyes fixed on the map of the United States of America, I waited till I could scrimp enough money to pay for a round-trip ticket and living expenses for a while in Chicago. At night the needle of my record player moved to the music of my Blues-master. Big Johnny White sang and played. And my guitar followed his, note for note, shade for shade.

Hit it, Big Johnny! Play it again. I'll see you soon in Chicago.

THREE

Christopher Columbus had scanned the ocean for days and days before that historic day when he discovered America. Since then, millions of men and women had made the voyage, and millions of others had dreamed of making it, not daring to set out for that New World, which, with its cowboys and Indians, its financial techniques and triumphs, its vast spaces, its innumerable eccentricities that we kept hearing about, was becoming more and more mythic, and more and more desirable. America. The great victor in the struggle against the Barbarians.

"God bless America!" my mother had never tired of saying during the darkest days of the storm.

And her prayer had been answered. God had blessed America, and the Americans had come, liberating, protecting, handing out chewing gum and chocolates, loaded with so many strange *gadgets* that the word itself stayed in our language, gadgets that would be the base of the super-consumer society which post-war America would spread throughout the world.

Among the Americans, there was Sugar, my tall

black friend. It was his America I had loved: the America of the Phantom and the Lone Ranger, of his gifts of friendship, of long rambles among the ruins, but more than anything, the America of the blues.

That was the America I set off to discover at a time when few Europeans and very few French were willing to undertake such an expensive trip.

I won't try to describe the excitement I felt, arriving at La Guardia Airport, the blunders of my first contacts, the sights I drank in with wide eyes, the too-long and too-expensive taxi rides, my first attempts to understand the customs and manners. After a few days in New York and a tip of the hat to the Statue of Liberty, whom I already knew from seeing her so often at the beginning of Columbia westerns, I felt I had sized up the New Continent, which really wasn't all that different and strange—pretty much the way it was in the movies—and was ready to move on to Chicago, the blues, and Big Johnny White, the real goal of my trip. As an old blues song endlessly repeated on one of my records:

> Come on, Baby, don't you want to go
> See the bright lights of my Sweet Home Chicago!

The bright lights were still lit in the heart of the city when the bus, dirty after a long night on the road, finally reached the city of Al Capone. It was still early, but the forest of skyscrapers was already coming to life: ultra-fast elevators were pouring out a flood of workers hurrying toward millions of anonymous cells, which soon would be clattering with typewriters and ringing with telephones.

At first sight Chicago didn't seem all that different from New York: the same spree of neon signs, the same wide sidewalks, the same lines of taxis filing by, the

34

tall buildings that covered the streets with a permanent shadow. But it wasn't New York, it was Chicago, and the most striking difference was the Elevated Metro, bewildering, omnipresent, insidious, asthmatic, swaying and lurching, skimming barely above the heads of the tallest pedestrians, with a squeaking of axles and a clanging of iron plates. What sinister architect had conceived the preposterous idea of that abominable heap of iron? Beneath the El there wasn't even shadow, just perpetual twilight, punctured here and there by the red neon signs of shops and snack-bars.

The pedestrians, reduced to shadows themselves, picked their way through a blackish labyrinth of sidewalks amputated of half their width by the iron infrastructure of the El. Suddenly the great legs of steel would tremble, the nuts and bolts break out dancing, the sidewalk undulate slightly from the vibrations; and the pedestrians would quicken their pace, their eyes shut and their heads bent forward against the shock, until the train had passed.

I wandered from expensive hotel to expensive hotel, not one of which, with my meager savings, I could afford, until I finally landed in one of those establishments common in the downtowns of American cities. It had been constructed as a luxury hotel at the turn of the century, but had gone to seed. The carpet was worn; the window panes opaque from never having been washed. A few septuagenarian porters carried the weariness of having done too much carrying. Next to the lobby, the cafeteria offered a semblance of food at moderate prices, not only for the hotel guest, but also for people in the neighborhood: the unemployed, beggars, newspaper venders, car washers, shoeshine boys and, by turns, the porters hungry after their sentry duty in the lobby. As the meal began, the clatter of forks and knives, the scraping of greasy dishes into the serving trays, and the ringing of the cash register, as it gulped down and spit out dollars and coins, made me think of a medieval beggars' colony. A crowd of old, sad rejects from American prosperity dragged their ragged silhouettes in a sleepwalk along the counter of dishes displayed for their appetite: boiled vegetables, ladles of indistinct broth, slices of bread. At the cash register, the customer would reach deep into the pocket of a worn pair of pants, pull out a few quarters and, once in a while, have to take a few awkward steps back to return a dish that exceeded his means.

Some unwritten law divided the room into clearly defined zones: blacks, old people, small-job holders. You could tell these last by the size of their platters. They chomped into their daily hamburgers, smothered in catsup. The old people chattered and babbled and stuffed themselves with memories of the good old days, gilded with time, and with bitter comments on the hard days now. Their eyes were fearful and eager in their wrinkled faces; their movements jerky as they plunged their spoons in and out of their broth and slurped noisily. After the meal, underfed faces opened to grotesque mouths, while shaky hands, armed with toothpicks, probed deep into them, scraping broken teeth, in search of some leftover.

I rang the receptionist's bell and she finally came to the counter. Her faded jeans did not conceal a single bulge. There was no friendliness in her voice as she checked the guest register. "That'll be seven dollars a night. Pay in advance!" When she saw the wad of bills I pulled out and counted with great care, her long, ant-like face, with its horn-rimmed glasses, relaxed a little, and she almost smiled as she handed me the key.

My room adjoined the lobby. The bed had worn

springs and sagged, the rug was riddled with cigarette holes, and the faucets dripped into a cracked-porcelain basin.

The thermostat didn't work right, and the air conditioner blew a continual blizzard of snow into the room. The television stood ready to bring me, at all hours, programs from the many local channels.

I pulled up the shade and looked out through the dirty panes. Night was falling on the badly-lit street. Big automobiles with leering faces were hurrying home to their suburbs. Above a little grocery store, a red neon sign with half the letters missing winked at me, but didn't tempt me. On the deserted sidewalk, an indistinct figure staggered toward the store. Soon he was under the sign, which spotlighted him for an instant. It was a half-drunk black man, a bottle in his hand.

I had found my America.

Listening to a blues record in a little room in Paris, with your nose pressed against a window dripping with rain—that was part of a mood, a melancholy, a despondency, but it was a melancholy that luxury permitted, the easy dejection you could afford to indulge in, because you had a full stomach and clean clothes. In Chicago, the blues were not just a music; they were the black ghetto.

Broken sidewalks, dilapidated Victorian brick houses with their broken windows scotch taped or replaced with cardboard, their doors caved in, cracks running down the sides of buildings, garbage bags burst open and overflowing into the gutted streets. Smelly concrete block buildings stood next to shacks nailed together with boards and roofed with corrugated tin. A few run-down stores fed an almost exclusively black population. The blues were the soul of these neighborhoods. They were everywhere: in the nightclubs, in the bars, and on the streets. The ragged children, running and laughing, the hundreds of prostitutes, pacing the street corners in their polished shoes, the drug pushers, the little old women in their thread-bare coats, carrying heavy grocery sacks, rummaging for riches in the trash, like gold miners of misery in a garbagey River Pactolus: these too were the blues. Professional gamblers who had gambled well, big shots who had climbed the ranks of the black mafia, and pimps, controlled the ghetto. With their spangled suits, their big, gaudy cars, shining with chrome, their impeccable white shoes, their heavy diamond and gold rings on every finger, their felt hats shoved down over dark faces, and their shiny white teeth glittering with gold, they were the territorial bosses. Nothing happened without them. No transaction escaped them. They were the police, the courts, the tax collectors, and the grantors of licenses.

The black ministers, both church pastors and street preachers, reigned over the spiritual world. Marvelous orators, excellent musicians, extraordinary exegetes of a Bible they knew to the smallest detail and interpreted according to their whim, they maintained a firm moral hold on the people. They were guides and commentators on the present, guardians of the past, bearers of hope for the future. Vice and Virtue thus shared governance over that poor society. This was how black America, consigned, pushed aside, and forgotten in the ghetto, lived.

I was at the Maxwell Street flea market, up to my elbows in old records. The blues echoed everywhere on the sidewalks. Street orchestras and guitarists strummed and sang with their bowls next to them. There were a few other whites there, too, Italians and Jews mostly, brothers in misery who hadn't been able to escape from the neighborhood.

But I was searching there for my holy grail.

For hours I had been sitting in one of those little cafes where they don't serve alcohol, clutching a big cup of American coffee that tasted of barley and listening to all the songs on the juke box. I had lost track of everything going on around me. Suddenly, a heavy weight on the bench where I was sitting jerked me out of my revery. One seated next to me and the other across from me, two impeccably dressed black men were looking me over, smiling. My coins were in my hand. My coffee, half drunk and half cooled, was in front of me. I didn't know what to do. I had been hanging around this neighborhood for days, careful at first, but with my guard lowered by now in the unaggressive atmosphere. At first I had been the object of vague curiosity, but after a while nobody paid any attention to me, and since my modest attire didn't arouse envy in anyone, I felt safe, walked around, came and went, listening everywhere to as much music as possible, and getting people to talk with me.

But now, trapped against the bawling juke box, I didn't know what attitude to adopt. A tenor sax, imprisoned in the coin machine, scraped the atmosphere, which was becoming more and more heavy as the two men watched me with ironic eyes. I decided not to do anything. What *could* I do? When the music stopped, one of the men spoke with a strong ghetto accent:

"What're you doin' here, Whitey?"

I spoke in the black accent I knew so well. This obviously surprised them. Gaining confidence, I told them that I had come from France, that I loved black music, that I played it myself, and that I was looking for a musician named Big Johnny White.

They weren't sure what to make of that. "You from the police?"

I started explaining all over again, that I was from France. . . .

"Fine, fine. . . . One question. What is this, this *France?* Is that a country or a town?"

When I said the word *Europe,* his eyes lit up: "Okay. All right."

I realized that here France is unknown. Only Europe exists.

A few more questions, some small talk, three steaming coffees brought by the waitress, a few words (incomprehensible to me), laughter, and the atmosphere relaxed.

Before leaving, they gave me some advice: "If you want to find that old guy that sings the blues, you better hit some of the clubs on the South Side."

They got up, and the one who had asked all the questions, lean and long and elegant in his three-piece gray pin-stripe suit, looked me over once more. "If anyone gives you any problems, tell 'em Ray says it's okay."

That incident saved me from lots of others. Ray's name was *open sesame* in the neighborhood. The bartenders protected me. The musicians I went to hear answered my questions. There in the ghetto all day long and a good part of the night, I got to be known as "the white boy from Europe who likes the blues."

More confident now and feeling sort of adopted, I ventured one step further and took my guitar to the Maxwell Street flea market. I tried to do it the way I had seen black musicians do it. A little nervous in spite of everything, I propped my back against a wall and tuned my guitar, taking longer than usual. Then, in the heart of the black Chicago ghetto, wedged timidly between a hot dog stand and a little market stall, I began to play the blues. My fingers moved about on the strings on their own, and I fixed my eyes on the neck of my guitar. I really wasn't eager to see what would happen. I hadn't gotten much good out of my last public appearance in Paris: a broken guitar and a few punches in the belly. Maybe I was just asking for trouble again.

A few long minutes went by. Little by little my fingers regained their habitual ease, running up and down the neck of the guitar. One after another, I reeled off the numbers in my repertoire: Muddy Waters, Robert Johnson, Big Johnny White. My eyes burned a hole in the guitar. At last I raised by head. To my surprise, a little semi-circle had formed in front of me: kinky-haired kids with badly-washed, grinning faces and patched sweaters; some men, too, in old leather coats, wide, shining, threadbare pants, and worn out shoes; and large, chattering women, shaking with laughter. And in my guitar case, which I had thrown down carelessly on the sidewalk beside me, lay several coins the poor blacks of the ghetto had left in homage to this musician who had come—one more, but so what, the more the merrier—to entertain them.

One tall man laughed and shouted, "Not bad, white boy, not bad! Play your blues, boy!"

All this aroused an intense emotion in me. It was an extraordinary moment. Suddenly I was known in a world I had loved without being able to touch, the way an archeologist loves the lost world he devotes his life to. But I, white and French, was living, here, in the heart of the Chicago ghetto, with my guitar in my hand, playing the blues. And black people appreciated me, encouraged me, paid me!

In France, there were beatings and contempt; here, friendship and welcome. Who was I really, and what world was I living in?

Everyone knew Big Johnny White, but no one knew where he was.

"You know," said the owner of a little club where I had been hanging out, "he goes back a long way. He's a real bluesman. He's got his guitar, and that's all he's got. He comes and goes. Maybe he's in St. Louis, Detroit, Cairo. . . . Maybe he's gone back South to get warm again. Or he could be in California. Could be in a Chicago jail, too. Never can tell about those guys. He's an old timer. They don't make 'em like that anymore."

Big Johnny White was unreachable. And the less I was able to find him, the more his music ran in my veins and urged me to look for him.

It was seven o'clock at night. As usual, the club was already half full. On a tiny stage, under weak lighting, a drum set was crowded between two big amplifiers. The rest of the room was filled with old round formica tables and a bunch of mismatched chairs: bar stools, folding chairs, lawn chairs, and along the walls, car seats for sofas.

Behind a bar that teetered under a pile of bottles, a slender black man in a yellow and black striped vest tended bar for a couple of dozen customers, all in their thirties or over. Young people didn't come to taverns like this anymore, where they could hear nothing but old blues songs. For them, the blues was old people's music, a patch of Southern countryside their parents had brought with them; they preferred more staccato rhythms, more sophisticated sounds, other messages and a new black soul, in what they were already calling soul music.

Four musicians were getting up on stage and plugging in their amplifiers. It was Wild Bill Jones's band. The drummer, well into his fifties, with a big round face and shiny gold teeth, barely managed to wedge himself between his bass drum and the wall. The leader, his white hair brushed back, wearing wire-rimmed glasses and a neat gray pin-striped suit, gripped his electric bass guitar against his stomach. One look from him and the band let loose with a boogie-woogie. It was greeted with applause from the group of drinkers.

I was at the bar, in front of a cold beer, watching the audience, poor farmers from Mississippi, Tennessee and Arkansas, with the mud still sticking to their shoes, poor sons of bitches who couldn't read or write. They had come to Chicago to drudge in factories. They huddled together with other home folks in clubs like these. The black ghetto was their new homeland of concrete and dilapidated buildings, but together they called up the South they had come from, adorned now with all virtues imaginable in the old homesick blues, which their friends and neighbors, like those crowded up there on the stage, played so well.

"*I'm goin' back down South . . .* ," Wild Bill sang, embracing the microphone.

And the drinkers swayed and laughed and called to the singer, "Why you wanna go South, Wild Bill?"

And he answered,

> *. . . 'cause that's where the sun shines every day.*
> *Goin' down South where the sun shines every day.*

The dialogue continued between the audience and the musicians.

"Come on, Wild Bill! Come on! Why you wanna go back down there?"

A smile, and he made up a new phrase:

Goin' South to my home and the land where the hens still lay.

A tall, thin young woman in a skin-tight dress burst out laughing and stood up: "You're holding something back on us, old boy. You got a girl down there! That's why you wanna go back!"

A moment of reflection, a phrase on the guitar, notes lashing out from tortured strings, and then Wild Bill answered, a malicious smile on the corners of his lips.

Goin' back where the women still got meat shakin' on their
*   bones!*

The crowd nodded their heads in delight, and the woman, still laughing though the line was obviously meant for her, sat down again with her friends.

Hours slipped by, and Wild Bill was still shaking the foundations of the fragile counter with his bass notes. His eyes were closed. A few drops of sweat pearled his temples. His head swayed, whitened by hard times, and his voice cracked from years of intense emotion. He kept reeling them off, one song after another.

I can't walk all alone, all alone down this dark road.

With heaving rhythms, the hypnotic guitar, the plaintive voice, and long moans as if from a deep wound, the Chicago blues became a little plot of earth torn from Mississippi soil.

My mamma died when I was young, when I was so awful
*   young.*
My mamma died when I was young, when I was so awful
*   young.*
She said, "Lord, have pity on my poor son, on my poor
*   son."*

Bill leaned on the end of his lines with lacerating falsettos. The silence in the room was absolute. Each person was living out the long anguish the singer had sung, and a few tears ran down the wrinkled, beat-up faces. It was three o'clock in the morning. I had hardly budged from my stool. I could feel my eyelids drooping.

The smoke was so thick it veiled the shadows thrown on the walls by the dim lights and stung my eyes. One last swallow of beer, and I was out on the sidewalk again. A fine drizzle was falling, and a cold wind was blowing from Lake Michigan. The chill air woke me up again, and I started back toward my hotel.

I had been walking for several minutes, my collar turned up against the cold, when suddenly I felt I was being followed. A glance over my shoulder told me I was right. Two men, in leather caps and jackets, were not far behind me. Their boots splashed a little in the puddles that were just beginning to form.

Up until now, I had wandered all over Chicago on foot, day and night, along the lake, in the fashionable areas, through the squares, and often in the ghetto, despite the advice of lots of people. Since I hadn't experienced danger, I had come to think of the "unsafe streets" everyone talked about as mythical. Or anyway highly exaggerated. I no longer paid any attention to what was going on around me, or rather, what wasn't going on. As my time in Chicago passed and my funds steadily dwindled, I had come to believe that my clothes, shabbier each day—my unironed jacket, unshined shoes, pants without any crease—couldn't offer the least temptation to muggers.

But obviously this evening, the late hour or the color of my skin or—who knows—a bad take during the day that could be made up for with a poor but easy take now, would change all that. This little side street had brought me into the path of the two thugs behind me, and I had a long way to go before I reached a larger street where I could hail a taxi, lose them in a subway stop, or take refuge in some all-night store or cafe. What could I do? Speed up, maybe, but they were used to running in these streets. They could probably catch me in no time, running on the broken-up sidewalks and streets, slaloming around the loose garbage. I decided to confront them.

I turned deliberately back toward them and shouted, trying to make my voice as firm as possible, "What do you want?"

They stopped. They obviously hadn't expected a reaction like that. I could see their tall figures and the clubs they had in their gloved hands. I wouldn't have a chance in a fight with them. A long, threatening moment passed. For the first time in my life, I was confronting real physical danger, and I found I wasn't the least bit afraid. They stood directly in front of me, ready to club me and strip me, and all I felt was a slight confusion from the strangeness of the situation and, crouched inside me, a faint, secret pleasure of being finally and truly in danger, of *living* danger and not just seeing it in a movie or reading about it in a book.

I repeated my question: "What do you want?"

They came a few steps closer. For an instant, we stood staring into each other's faces. They were two big old boys, that's all. In any other circumstances, I wouldn't even have noticed them.

I looked them in the eye. "I don't have much. I'm broke."

I could see the one on the right grip his club tighter and raise it slightly. "Your watch, your belt, your wallet."

They took another step toward me, then two. They looked more and more threatening. I unclasped my watch and took my wallet out of my pocket. With a quick movement, I slipped my driver's license out, because I didn't want to lose it, too. I undid my leather belt. In a second, they were on me. I could see their white eyes in faces the night made even blacker. Red filaments striped their pupils. They tore the watch, wallet and belt from my hands.

"The ring, too!" the one on the right shouted, pointing at the little silver-plated circle I had been wearing for years. I took it off and gave it to him.

The other one was exploring my wallet. I could tell he was disappointed.

"I told you I didn't have much," I said in a calm voice.

They looked me over once more for what seemed like an eternity.

"Your coat," the first guy said, already tugging at my sleeve.

I gave it to him. Far off, a car was turning onto the deserted street.

They had their trophies, wretched spoils for two miserable thugs, and they started off, brandishing their clubs. Two, three, four steps backward, and suddenly they turned tail and took off as fast as they could. By the time the car reached the spot where I was standing, they had disappeared around the corner.

I didn't even bother waving at the car. The white headlights blinded me for a second, and the car brushed by me, splashing my shoes. For an instant, the red taillights glistened in the night, and then the car was gone. In my shirt sleeves, my feet wet, dripping with rain, shivering from the cold, I set out once more through the dark toward my hotel.

I had to move. Even my second class hotel had become too expensive. From then on I paid by the week for a room near Roosevelt Road, on the edge of the ghetto. Poles, Greeks, Czechs, Jews, Italians, some blacks, and some half-starved wretches of Irish extraction shared the building. They were the déclassés of the consumer society, non-producers in a system consecrated to production, workers out of work still dreaming of regaining their place in life, and newly-arrived immigrants. We passed on the stairs without a word, only a brief meeting of eyes that said volumes. A spigot in the corridor of each floor brought us together sometimes in the morning. In our undershirts, holding our razors, we waited in line, exchanging one or two sentences, banalities in all tones and accents. Some had fled repressive regimes or overpopulation where there wasn't enough food. Others had lost everything, and this poor building was their last stage before the streets. They passed each other in the shaky stairwells, in the dusty corridors, next to the cold water spigot. And I was in the middle of them, with my return-trip ticket to France in my pocket, going neither up nor down. Nowhere.

To get by, I had to take on some small jobs, on the sly because I didn't have a work permit. My guitar playing brought in a few pennies that I stretched as far as possible. I unloaded crates at the grain markets on La Salle Street, cleaned rifles at the armory. But generally, no one wanted to hire me. I had been to the Chicago Public Library to try to get work there because, after all, my only credentials were my work at the National Library. Besides, with a stable, honorable employment there, I might be able to obtain a Permanent Resident's card. But they didn't need me: a Japanese, a Chinese, an Indian, a Slav, a specialist in some other exotic literary language, perhaps, but not a Frenchman whose only other language was English.

By now I knew Chicago by heart and I had had enough of it. Enough of the broad, straight avenues where you never met anyone on foot. Enough hamburgers. Enough of the dingy room I rented. Enough even of the ghetto, in spite of the kindness of the people, in spite of the blues. The thought of returning to France was growing more and more appealing. Even so, I still would have liked to meet Big Johnny White and tell him, "I've come all this way to meet you! I've listened to you so much, I've played along with you so often, I've learned so much from you that I wanted to see you and thank you." I had seen and experienced lots in Chicago, but he remained as distant as ever.

The owner of one little shop with books and records piled all around told me, "You know, he could be dead somewhere—who knows where? And we'd learn about it in a month or maybe a year!"

More days went by, with no luck. I decided to leave. What was I doing there?

I was buying a few things in a supermarket when a tall figure, speaking loudly to one of the sales clerks, caught my attention. That height, that face, those hands, that thick warm voice? Before me, just a few feet away, stood Sugar. He had aged and put on some weight. His shoulders were stooped a little on his great body. His hair had whitened considerably. But there was no doubt about it. There he was. Sugar!

As he was leaving, pushing a big grocery cart in front of him, I caught his eye and smiled. "Sugar! Remember me?"

Astonished, he opened his eyes wide the way I had often seen him do. A slight shake of his head told me that he didn't recognize me.

"Your buddy, Sugar! Ten years ago. The American base, our long walks, *le port*, Thérèse!"

Now he remembered.

"Come on home with me! We've got to celebrate this!"

He was a taxi driver, and it was in his taxi, an old patched-up rattletrap, that we went to his home. It was some distance, a little into the southern suburbs, beyond the ghetto but close to its boundaries. He lived in

49

a little apartment in a drab brick building. Up a flight of creaking stairs he ushered me in, laughing, and went into the kitchen to look for a bottle.

The room was a terrible mess. Old armchairs, once leather, were barely visible under an assortment of odd objects. A chest of drawers stood unsteadily on three legs, spilling multicolored clothes from its open drawers. On the floor, a plastic floor covering was smothered under dirty shirts, pajama tops and bottoms, and underwear. On the wall was a large, yellowing photograph of him in uniform, taken somewhere in Europe during the war. The Age of Glory.

He came back in, carrying two fairly clean glasses in one hand and a bottle of scotch in the other.

"We're going to celebrate this."

But his strained exuberance faltered at my questioning look. I had known him as a sergeant in the Army of Liberation. He had been tall then, strong, impeccable in his uniform, and the world he brought me had been extraordinarily attractive, an America that was overwhelming, kind, and protective, exactly what he had been in my life, my great friend Sugar.

So was it all just a mirage, a marvelous oasis I had been running toward all my life only to discover, when I finally reached it today, that it was just a little patch of sand? And dirty, cold sand you wouldn't want to walk on in bare feet.

Sugar, my friend, who had given me so much and whom I had loved so much, was there, and he understood my look, his arms slack, the empty glasses in his hand. He cleared off the armchairs as best he could, and we managed to sit down.

"Yeah," he said, "this ain't so hot. I should have stayed in the Army."

Somewhere in the building—downstairs, upstairs—

someone put on a record. It was James Brown, the blacks' new idol then. Over violins and electric guitar arpeggios, the brasses behind him, with his powerful, lightly muffled preacher's voice, James Brown delivered his message: *It's a ma-aan's world.*

Sugar talked softly about his wife, how she had left him, taking all their savings. He had looked for her but never found her. She might be somewhere in California, near her family.

"I tell you, old man," he sighed and drank some of his whiskey, "she was one sweet mamma! She really did get under my skin. It gave me a hell of a shock when she left me like that!"

Outside, buses passed in the late afternoon gloom. James Brown went on with his sermon:

> *Man made little boys.*
> *And then he made them some toys.*

Sugar shook his head. He had a son somewhere, too. The boy had up and left one day, just like his mamma.

"He sent me two or three letters. After that, pff . . . nothing." He took another drink and repeated the word several times: ". . . nothing."

A man and a woman, already tipsy, made the stairwell landing creak. The man was talking fast and the woman was laughing. James Brown was still singing.

> *Man made cars. Man made planes.*

Sugar bent his great head over his glass. A patch of brown skin showed through his prematurely white hair.

"That's life, boy. One day you got everything— money, a woman, a kid. Next day, nothing."

Somewhere, somebody was urinating loudly. A pause. Then a toilet flushed. I could hear the traffic was getting heavier. The violins reached a crescendo. The guitar spun out its dramatic reel, and James Brown shouted:

Man made everything. He made everything.

The brasses filled the air.

But he ain't got nothing, he ain't got nothing
If he hasn't got a woman or a girl.

Sugar was there before me, physically present, occupying a space in his own world. But where was the soldier, the liberator, the friend, the big brother, the initiator?

Sugar aged, Sugar bleached, Sugar broken, poor old Sugar. Was it possible? Maybe I was dreaming. The rain was beginning to fall on the building's yellowed windows. We could hear neighbors laughing, talking, eating. Somewhere a door slammed. A child was being scolded and was sassing back.

And now here was Sugar, real and sad, and cold. No Phantom or Lone Ranger was going to rescue him. He wasn't in danger, just alive. He had taken off his uniform. His black face was beginning to wrinkle. The Phantom and the Lone Ranger had taken off their masks, too.

I said a long goodbye to Sugar, clapping him on the shoulder. We'd see each other again, sure, but in France, in the next war, because I was leaving Chicago and going back home. We shook hands hard. He was glad he had seen me again, he said. I hesitated as I started to leave, and his eyes met mine a last time: the same look as before, lively, intense, kind, but now I read something else there. He closed the door quietly. The stairs moaned as I went down.

Somewhere in the distance, James Brown took up his

refrain again: *It's a man's man's world. It's a ma-aan's world. . . .*

I had paid my rent and handed in my keys. The bus for New York was leaving in the late afternoon, so I still had several hours to spend in Chicago. Almost mechanically I returned one last time to the Southside ghetto. The dilapidation, the little shops, the laughter of the ragged children were all familiar to me now. I greeted some of the shopkeepers that I had come to know. "I'm leaving," I told them.

"Oh, yeah," they said, "everybody goes back home some day." We exchanged a little small talk. I walked for a long time, one of the rare whites among a multitude of blacks, but they had gotten used to seeing me there.

I stepped into the little cafe where I had met Ray and his henchman. That had been only a few weeks before, but it seemed like an eternity. The manager and some customers were arguing about something. I sat down in my favorite corner, next to the juke box. The plastic seat had been slashed, and tufts of kapok were hanging out. I knew the list of songs by heart. I had listened to them all, some of them dozens of times. 32A was Big Johnny White singing his version of "Sweet Home Chicago." I slid a coin into the slot, and Big Johnny began with the light, velvety strumming he did so well. The drummer was puffing hard to keep up. Now Big Johnny was singing:

> *One and one is two. Two and two is four.*
> *Come on up here, baby. You're gonna get lots more!*
> *My sweet home, Chicago!*

I read over the song titles one last time. Suddenly a large form interposed between the ceiling light and the jukebox.

I turned abruptly. All I could see at first was a great belly, with two buttons missing on the fly of a shabby pair of pants, held up by speckled suspenders.

I raised my eyes. A huge black man, bulging fat, was standing before me. A faded Stetson was crammed down over his head.

When I looked into his staring eyes, he said, "I hear you been looking for me all over town. I'm Big Johnny White."

FOUR

Big Johnny White was sitting down and I was talking to him. I was trying to explain why I had come, about his records, about my guitar, the blues, Europe. Excited, sensing that I was living out a great encounter, I talked.

He didn't. He wore a red and black checkered shirt. His broad-brimmed cowboy hat hid the expression on his round and wrinkled face. He sat there, bent over slightly, his hands folded.

Minutes passed. My flood of words was slowing to a trickle. I had told him everything now.

How many times I had imagined this encounter! He would marvel that anyone could have come from so far in search of him. He would be flattered that anyone loved his records and his music enough to cross the Atlantic and spend weeks searching the ghetto from one end to the other in the hope of finding him. Then he would take up his guitar and play one of his songs for me. For me.

But now he kept quiet, didn't move, waited. The customers came and went, drank and talked. They had no idea of any historic encounter.

At last he opened his mouth: "I'm thirsty. I don't talk when I'm thirsty." He swallowed his syllables in a Southern drawl.

I asked him what he wanted to drink.

"Whiskey, Jim Beam."

They didn't serve whiskey where we were, or at that time of the morning anywhere else in Chicago, or maybe anywhere else in the United States of America. I told him that. He didn't flinch. A new silence set in.

"Give me five dollars," he finally muttered.

I dug into my pockets and handed him a five dollar bill.

He rose without a word, his belly shaking the table.

"Order me a cup of coffee and wait here." With heavy steps he walked out of the cafe.

The hot coffee was on the table when he came back a few minutes later, carrying a package. He took off his Stetson, and for the first time I could see his hazel eyes, circled with heavy wrinkles. With fingers like sausages he gripped the cup and gulped the coffee down. He wiped the bottom of the cup with his index finger and hid the cup under the table, where he filled it with whiskey. He recorked the bottle and folded the brown paper discreetly around it again. "Now," he said, "I'm listening. What do you want?"

I hesitated. I couldn't understand exactly what was going on in his head. I started over, explaining why I had come, how I loved his records, how I had learned his chords.

He drank from his cup in little sips.

Again I came to the end of my explanation. Again, silence. As he filled his cup again, he said without looking at me, "You want me to cut a record? That's twenty dollars a song. Pay in advance."

He went back to sipping the alcohol. I was baffled. Somewhere there was a connection missing. I tried to explain that I was not a record producer and that I just wanted to meet him because I liked his music, that he was the best in the world.

"You want to take me on tour in Europe? John Lee Hooker and T-bone Walker went." He chuckled scornfully and went on sipping. "There's money over there, wine, pretty girls."

He laughed softly. "I'm an old man. I'm an old man."

I looked at his wrinkled forehead, the crow's-feet around his eyes, his thick fingers and the masses of flesh bulging everywhere through his clothes, and figured he was into his seventies.

He kept talking between whiskeys. "I never been up in a plane. That would be nice, go overseas before I die."

I had come to him with my ears dazzled with his music, my heart full of his blues, a student to an unknown master. And here was an old black man, drinking his whiskey and asking me for a last wish. I thought of my meeting the night before with Sugar. Big Johnny's cowboy hat cast a shadow on the table. A strange emotion gripped me.

"I'll try," I said. "Where can I find you?" Then I added, "Where can I hear you play?"

He got up, a big barrel in tight pants.

"I'm goin' South tonight," he said. "Meet me at the Greyhound station at six."

Without another look, his enormous body unsteady, he lumbered out, his package pressed against his shirt.

The Greyhound station had been my first experience of Chicago. Today it would be my last. It was a vast hall with a few shops, a cafeteria, and rows of chairs welded together. Hundreds of passengers were waiting around, sleeping, reading, watching the portable televisions that were fixed onto their stands. There would be several buses I could catch for New York. But I was also waiting for Big Johnny White, wondering what he wanted with me, wondering whether he would even show up.

Seven o'clock. The next bus for New York was at eight-thirty. I decided to wait till then. Outside, a frozen wind was still blowing and it was beginning to drizzle again. People were coming in and going out, letting in the cold air. I curled up tighter in my old raincoat, pressed my baggage against my feet, and dozed.

Someone was shaking my shoulder. I woke up to find Big Johnny standing over me in his white hat and his red and black checked shirt, with his stomach protruding over his pants. He was carrying a battered guitar case.

"Let's go," he said.

I shook the sleep out of my head and leaped up.

"You got the tickets?" he asked.

Again I was stupefied.

"What tickets?"

"For Clarksdale. We change at Memphis. The bus leaves in a quarter hour."

I didn't react. I stood with my arms hanging slack, looking at him, in the middle of the Chicago bus station, in his odd getup and a guitar case covered with bumper stickers.

"If you want to hear me play," he grumbled, "that's where I play. . . . Go get two tickets for Clarksdale."

It dawned on me now, plain and clear: Big Johnny White wanted me to pay his return trip South; then he would play for me. I didn't produce records, he didn't believe I could arrange a tour in France for him, but I wanted to hear him play. This was the price.

For a few seconds I stood rooted on this crossroads of my life, not knowing which direction to take. Eastward was New York, my plane for France, probably the end of my American adventure, and then what? A long wait for retirement. Southward was Mississippi, the land of the blues, and Big Johnny White at home, in the heart of his world. Maybe I still had enough money to get there and back. Almost without thinking what I was doing, I went to the window and bought two tickets for Clarksdale.

A few minutes later, we were on the bus. Big Johnny put his guitar on the baggage rack and squeezed into the window seat. His huge body didn't leave me a lot of room. The bus was full, so there wasn't anything to do but squeeze into what was left of the seat beside him.

As the bus pulled out, I got ready to make conversation with him, but his broad-brimmed hat was shoved down over his eyes and his hands were folded on his belly. He was sleeping. A few more jolts down the highway, and he was snoring.

It was a long voyage on a straight line, down through the flat country. Night enveloped the bus, driven by a tall, middle-aged man in a grayish brown uniform, always "careful, confident and courteous," as the sign above the windshield promised. Little by little the talk died down and the hum of the bus took over, insidious, penetrating, cradling. We nodded, we dozed, we slept. We lost all measure of time. Sometimes glaucous lights would go on and the engine would stop. Into the watercolor gray of a Greyhound station the bus would pour its flood of passengers. Stove up, rumpled, their eyes red from sleep, they stumbled out in search of coffee to rinse their pasty mouths or a bland sandwich to line their hollow stomachs. Sometimes you could hear travelers who were leaving the bus saying their goodbyes. A handshake, a few friendly words, a name that would be quickly forgotten, and one of them would disappear in the night, no longer a face, not yet a shadow. Someone else would take the seat, more banalities would be exchanged, the hum would take over again, and heads would rock against the backs of the tall seats.

Bloomington, Springfield, Evansville, one name after another, all alike, glimpses of shacks and shanties, another bus station. Roadsigns. The sky was clear now. Not one tree threw its sooty shadow across the night. There was only an immense plain. Since Chicago, Big Johnny White hadn't budged. I fell into a deep sleep.

Again he woke me. He was trying to get past me, but it was impossible for him to lift his leg around me. I got up to let him out. I thought he wanted to go to the bathroom, but he pulled his guitar down from the baggage rack. The bus was still moving, so I knew he wasn't getting off. Without a look, without a word, without a gesture, he walked to the back of the bus and made room for himself as best he could, shoving and pushing the stomachs and hips of the sleepers.

His complete disregard for me was beginning to get on my nerves. After dragging me off on this dangerous expedition—that I was paying for—he decides he doesn't like my company. Well, *Monsieur* Big Johnny White! I could see him back there, about to shove his ridiculous cowboy hat back down over his eyes and go to sleep again.

In four strides I was on him: "What's the matter? I was bothering you perhaps?"

60

The anger in my voice threw him off. It was his turn to be surprised. For the first time, his eyes were wide open. Drawling his words more heavily than ever, he said, "My boy, we're coming into Kentucky. This is the South now."

I still didn't see what he was getting at, so he added in a low voice, "You're white. You stay up front. I don't want any scenes!"

With that, Big Johnny put his Stetson back over his face and folded his hands over his stomach again. Around him, all the other sleepers were black, too. It was beginning to get light outside. I went back to my seat.

It was late afternoon when we reached Memphis. October was almost over, but the weather was still very pleasant. What a contrast with Chicago, with its cold wind off Lake Michigan and its never-ending frozen drizzle. Memphis! A magic word. The city of Elvis and rock 'n' roll, the home of W. C. Handy, who used to play on Beale Street. And the Mississippi River, "long, wide, and deep," rolling its muddy waters along the docks where the cotton boats had discharged their cargo for so many years.

We had a few hours' layover before the bus to Clarksdale. In a sleazy cafe where Big Johnny sat by himself at a table across the room from me, we ate a couple of quick hamburgers. "I don't like Memphis," he said twice, when I went over and urged him to get out of the cruddy place where he seemed glued to the chair.

So I set out on my own. It was after five o'clock, and Main Street was deserted. Some beggars were hanging around the adjacent streets, accosting without much conviction the few hurried passers-by. The beggars came and went in little groups, exchanging scraps of information and picking newspapers out of the trash.

A pint-sized raggamuffin came bounding out at me from a Woolworth's entrance. I could read disappointment on his face when he saw how rumpled and disheveled I was after twenty hours on the Greyhound. No, I didn't want to buy the newspaper he was half-heartedly offering me, one he had picked up a few minutes earlier.

A few more blocks and suddenly I was there. The Mississippi lay before me. It had been waiting for me, that big, good old river, indifferent to bus schedules for Clarksdale. The wharf, a large, now half-empty parking lot, sloped toward the water; three paddle-wheel boats were docked there, in a kaleidoscope of colors, bearing the names of provocative women: *Memphis Queen, Belle Star, Mississippi Queen.*

The sun was beginning to set, throwing its oblique rays on the water. The river, despite the songs that call it muddy, was a brilliant blue.

I hurried to get back to the station. I had seen Memphis.

Big Johnny was exactly where I had left him, slouched in front of his empty cardboard plate. He had fallen asleep again. It was time to leave for Clarksdale. This time it was I who woke him.

Without a word, he went to the back of the bus, and this time I didn't say anything. We were on the road again.

A few more hours and we had finally arrived. I was in the heart of Mississippi, in the heart of the blues, in the presence of Big Johnny White! It was something I would never have dreamed possible a few days before. But now I was hardly even excited. Worn out, rumpled, stiff, I wasn't even sure what I had come for. And this fat black man in his greasy shirt, with his fly never closed all the way and his beat-up old guitar case, was this really Big Johnny White? My Big Johnny White?

"I'll be playing at Lula's tonight," he told me, standing in front of the shack that served as a bus station. Then he turned to go. I was getting angry again. Oh, no! It wasn't going to be like that. I said I was going with him whether he liked it or not.

"My boy," he told me, "You'll find me at Lula's. Lula's waiting for me. And she's waiting *alone*."

He muttered some address I couldn't understand. I rummaged in my suitcase and pulled out a pencil and paper.

"Here," I ordered. "Write down where I can find you."

"I can't." He was getting impatient. He was going to eat with Lula. He was probably going to do other things with Lula. He was going to play the guitar at Lula's, and me, I was in the way.

"Why can't you?" I asked.

"I can't write."

Big Johnny White, the man who had taught me such marvelous music, had to burrow at the back of a bus and didn't know how to read and write. He repeated Lula's address, and I wrote it down as best I could. Then he went off without another look at me, his shirt tail sticking out the back of his pants and flapping to the beat of his elephant-like walk. I had to go to the bathroom in the little building next to the station. One sign above the doors read "White"; the other, "Colored."

A few black silhouettes came and went with hurried or hesitating steps under the pale light of the bulbs that lit the street. Some of the stores were beginning to close. Cafes and bars were beginning to open. I walked a few hundred yards on Grand Street, the only white shadow in the black ghetto of Clarksdale, and turned left after three blocks.

However bad the lighting was on Grand Street, it was flood light compared to what the sidewalk lamps gave me to see my way by now. Some half-starved, mangy dogs ran up to sniff my heels as I looked for the house number Big Johnny had given me. I advanced cautiously up the dark, dirt sidewalk, past greasy papers and cardboard boxes, around the large, ominous forms of half-emptied trash cans, which I sometimes bumped into.

The street was nothing but two lines of broken-down shacks facing each other. Many of the window panes had been replaced with newspapers. Front steps were caved in. Old car seats served as porch chairs.

Here and there American cars that had survived long years of use stood, big and gaudy, in front of the cracked façades of the houses. I could hear children playing football in a field nearby. Music was pouring out from everywhere, staccato rhythms, tidy riffs of the soul music of James Brown and Otis Redding, the hot black voices of the idols of the moment. Laughter and snatches of conversation spilled from the dilapidated porches, then stopped as I passed, an unwanted white silhouette rising from a confusion of late-twilight shadows, deliberately it seemed, asking for trouble in the poor black man's world. Who was the white man walking in the ghetto? In Clarksdale, no white ever walked in the ghetto.

Sometimes I caught remarks I understood the sense of, if not the exact words. Remarks meant for me, followed by laughter. I breathed a sigh of relief when I made out the dim light of a little cafe up ahead, and underneath the light, in proud gold letters, *Lula's*.

Superb music floated out the windows and through the plank walls. Velvety notes coiled upward. In a thick, rich voice, a little frayed with age, fatigue, and alcohol, Big Johnny White was singing. I pushed the door open. A metal tube shone on his left ring finger, which he slid up and down the metal strings of his old guitar. His big fingers tore out astonishing chords. His eyes were half closed. Sweat ran down his forehead, still capped by that same old cowboy hat.

> *Turn down your light, baby. Baby, turn down your light.*
> *Turn down your light, baby. Baby, turn down your light.*
> *I'm gonna stay here, gonna stay here all night.*

An acrid smoke enveloped him and the blacks of all ages that crowded around him, laughing, drinking, and dancing. For a short while, Big Johnny continued alone. A few more exquisite notes, then he, too, saw me, and he stopped playing. He spoke to a plump little black woman, all belly and rear end, whose face retained some beauty behind her atrocious, red plastic glasses. He leaned over and spoke to her, but everybody heard him: "He's a friend—come with me from Chicago to hear me play."

Lula riled up: "I don't want no whites here! 'Specially no northern whites. I don't want no problems!"

Big Johnny calmed her down with a wave of his hand. "He's not white. He's French. He's from Europe."

Lula and everybody else in the place looked at me with astonishment. Big Johnny was already playing again, this time a fast boogie. Little by little they took their eyes off me. If I wasn't white, well. . . . Again the glasses were emptied and filled. Again the bodies danced. I sat down in a corner and made myself as inconspicuous as possible.

I'm so alone and I got the blues so bad
I'm so alone and I got the blues so bad
I even hear the wind at my door cryin' sad.

The more Big Johnny told us of his long struggle against the lonesomeness that surrounded him and beat against his door, the deeper he drowned in the blues. His feet beat time, his fingers stroked the strings and vibrated with his gelatinous stomach, making the guitar whack up and down. The guitar was worn with years and beaten by travel. Its wood was peeling, and it was patched with adhesive tape. Big Johnny White's pupils were dilated; his body sweated incessantly. The others shouted and challenged him. He uttered a long moan, punctuated with passionate notes.

The heat had become unbearable. Lula wet her lips with some whiskey out of the bottle, then carried it to Big Johnny's mouth. He drank long, still playing his guitar, took up his song again, then drank again. All the feet were beating time on the wood floor. Bodies mingled. Beer cans disappeared. The bottle of whiskey passed from hand to hand, from mouth to mouth, a generous burst of life quickly swallowed, a fiery kiss that brought all souls together. The faces changed with the song. Glad songs, sad songs, slow and fast songs: an immense repertoire, sung for his own people, for himself, a black man among black people. Everyone had drunk too much, smoked too much, danced too much. There was muffled laughter, the swishing of dresses, the clanking of bottles, big smiles, gold teeth shining in the dim light. The air was suffocating. The whiskey and smoke burned my throat till I couldn't stand it any longer. I stepped outside the cafe to get a breath. As if she had been waiting for me, the Mississippi moon rose suddenly at the end of the street. With her good old yellow face, she had come to shine a spotlight on Miss Lula's cafe.

When I woke, it was broad daylight. Worn out from the long trip and drunk from cigarette smoke and vapors of alcohol, I had fallen asleep at the back of the cafe, flat on the floor, with my suitcase for a pillow. I had expected to snooze a couple of minutes, but the night had passed without my hearing another thing, not the shouts nor the laughter, not Big Johnny singing, not the people leaving.

With one leap I was up. The room was empty, but someone was moving about in the next room, and a smell of coffee filled the air. I knocked at the door the noise was coming from. A woman's voice answered something I couldn't understand, but which I took to mean, "Come in." I pushed the rickety door open.

Lula was standing at an old stove in a pink and mauve bathrobe, her head bristling with colored hair curlers. She looked back and threw me a ghost of a smile: "You ain't left yet?"

I didn't know what to say. No, I hadn't left. Up until then, my main accomplishment had been getting there, which in the cold light of morning seemed a lot. I stammered some polite thanks for the hospitality and asked her if I could have a cup of coffee.

"Sure." She poured a cup and handed it to me. She watched me drink. I could tell she was intrigued. After a minute, she asked me. "Are you really not white?"

I couldn't help laughing. "If Big Johnny told you I wasn't. . . ."

As if on cue, Big Johnny emerged from somewhere in the back of the cafe. From his heavy walk, I could tell he had already had his morning dose of whiskey. He sat down opposite me without saying a word. But I was used to that. I kept drinking my coffee. Lula brought Big Johnny a cup. He gulped the burning liquid down in one swill, then he said to Lula, "Pass me the bottle."

She grumbled a few anti-alcoholic sentiments, but went into the kitchen and brought him back a big demijohn of whitish-yellowish liquid without any label on it. He poured himself one cup and downed it without flinching; then a second. I had finished my coffee, and suddenly the alcohol looked powerfully tempting. Maybe that's what a man needed to sing the blues.

"Want some?" he said, and he filled my cup.

I drank, and a terrible fire invaded my throat, scorched my palate, and flamed up into my nostrils. It was poison! Burning alcohol! I coughed and pushed the cup back.

Lula burst out laughing. Big Johnny looked at me, amused. "Your moonshine don't agree with him, Lula," he said.

They talked with each other about people, things, and places I had never heard of. Their English was sewn with private expressions that were hard for me to make sense of. Their Southern accent and black idioms mixed in a sort of *patois* a long way from the language of the Chicago ghetto.

I sat stuck there with nothing to do. I don't know what I was expecting. As far as my two hosts were concerned, I no longer existed. Big Johnny kept on drinking; it was impressive to watch how much of that awful stuff he could put down. At last I managed to ask him, when Lula left to go into the kitchen or somewhere else in the house, "What are you going to do now?"

From out of the wrinkles in his sockets, he fixed me with a malevolent eye. "I'm goin' fishin', Whitey."

It was the first time he had called me that, and it was probably not a good omen. The tone of his voice wasn't friendly, either; no doubt I should have left him in peace, but I kept at him.

"Are you staying in Clarksdale, or going somewhere else?"

He didn't answer me. Instead he took the bottle and filled himself another cup. That must have been the tenth, at least. His arm had gotten shaky, and he spilled as much whiskey as he poured.

I asked him again, and he glared at me murderously. His fingers were having trouble gripping the cup. They were swollen. I was sure that if I had shaken his hand at that moment I would have squeezed a puddle of whiskey onto the table.

His voice was hoarse and slurred. "I don't like people askin' me questions."

He tried to get up. He was heavy, enormous, unsteady, an old, sick man, disheveled, alcoholic, ignorant, coarse, half-civilized even. But what civilization was I thinking about? The one that separated blacks from whites even at the urinals? Here Big Johnny White was in his own world, and even if he was eaten up by whiskey, even if he was a bum or a tramp, he was still the spokesman for his people. He made them laugh, weep, sing and dance. He was an artist of immense stature, a magnificent bluesman. His records, which I had played and replayed in my little room in Paris, had drawn me all the way to the heart of these black boondocks in the center of Mississippi. Big Johnny White had taught me the blues.

But this wasn't the Big Johnny White I had imagined. The only time he was, was when he was playing the guitar. That's why he played it. Without it, he was just a poor, fat illiterate son of a bitch without an income, without a home, whose only passion was whiskey. But that was what generated the music. Across the months of initiation with Sugar and my years of listening to records and playing the guitar, I had longed to know where the music came from. Now I knew. Now I saw.

Big Johnny White was staggering, trying to step forward. His enormous body weighed down with alcohol, misshapen from fat, seemed to weigh tons. I was suddenly overwhelmed with pity. And tenderness. This poor wretch, trying to put one huge foot in front of the other, this bum, was the artist whose music had sweetened my blue evenings, who had taught me so much, who had led me this far. That music had opened a new world for me. It had made me aware of a humanity whose misery I had never understood. The sound of the guitar scraped by a broken bottle neck, subtle, magical, was bound to that groping shape, hanging onto the table in a struggle to stay upright. The guitar was drenched in alcohol. That was the secret. Beauty was fat, dirty, and ragged. Big Johnny White was complete.

He let go his grip on the edge of the table, tried to move forward, and swayed for an instant on his big feet. He was about to fall. Without thinking, I leapt up and stood by his side to sustain him, aid him, guide him where he wanted to go. At that instant, I felt an irrepressible affection for him.

But he didn't share my feeling. With a fling of his right arm he sent me flying. My back struck a sharp corner of the table. I felt an intense pain and let out a brief cry. He turned toward me, all of a sudden solid and sturdy on the two legs that a moment before had threatened to collapse beneath him. His eyes fixed upon me with the cold light of hatred, and his hand grasped a switchblade produced from I don't know where. He moved toward me with murder in his hand and in his eye. I recovered enough presence of mind to dodge his swing and scramble behind the table. A burning sensation made me look down at my shirt. He had cut me. He kept coming, heavy but implacable, his knife still in his hand.

"I wasn't trying to harm you!" I cried.

He growled some sentences I could only half understand. "I've had all I can take from you, honky. I don't like people following me around, stickin' to me."

The blade was gleaming in his hand, with red at the steel point. I felt my chest. It was sticky with blood. I grabbed up a chair.

"I'm going to have your skin, white trash!" For a moment, I thought I had had it. I was going to die in this backwater corner of Mississippi, my body lying in a pool of blood on the worm-eaten floor of this crummy cafe, killed by a big drunk in the middle of an alcoholic fit.

I ran toward the kitchen and called, "Lula, help!" I was dripping blood now.

He shouted more insults and, with a loud cry, slashed the space between us. He thrashed the air, once, twice, three times, then he threw himself upon me. I held the chair up like a shield, but I didn't have to use it. Carried forward by its own momentum, his enormous body suddenly unhinged. He tottered once more, then toppled to the floor a few inches from me, nose down, his huge gut cushioning his fall. His knife slid from his hand and out of his reach. A slow second elapsed. I held my breath, my hands clutching the chair. Blood was pouring through my shirt, staining the floor. I felt faint. Big Johnny White stayed down, nose to the floor, his cowboy hat still stuck to his head. A few seconds, and from his thick carcass came a heavy, rhythmic grinding noise. He was snoring.

I dropped the chair and opened the door to the kitchen. I tried to yell, but I couldn't. Suddenly my legs gave way and I, too, crumpled to the floor. Before losing consciousness, I heard the hurried footsteps of Lula coming back from nowhere.

When I woke up I was laid out on a narrow wood bed. Lula was there, worried and attentive. At a glance I took in the bedroom, its faded wallpaper, threadbare rug, and dried flowers. On the wall was a display of pictures, photographs of John Kennedy, and photos of Lula herself at various ages, some with her family. Above them all, in an elaborate gold frame, hung an autographed sepia portrait of Martin Luther King. She brought me some kind of hot broth, which I quickly drank.

"Everything's gonna be all right," she told me.

She bustled all around me, explaining that while I was unconscious she had called in one of her friends, a healer of sorts. I had lost some blood but Big Johnny's knife hadn't gone very deep.

That evening I was up without any problems, and I thanked Lula for taking such good care of me. She still looked anxious.

"You won't say anything to the police?" she asked.

If I had been a black man, it probably wouldn't have mattered very much, but a white man cut up in a black cafe in the middle of Mississippi—that would have been blood of a different color. I reassured her that I had no intention of going to the police. All I needed was a clean shirt.

Lula gratified me with a broad smile. Then she rummaged through a rickety stand-up closet, smelling of potpourri, and pulled out a bright yellow shirt. As I tried it on, she told me it had belonged to one of her four sons. None of them had stayed South. They were in Chicago, St. Louis, or Detroit, she wasn't too sure: she didn't get word from them very often. Sometimes they'd come back, stay a few weeks, go fishing and hunting, and then they'd leave, forget to take one of their shirts or a pair of pants. She washed anything that was left behind, ironed it, and kept it like a relic. She had never been married, and she was alone now. This cafe was all she had. She laughed, suddenly happy and talkative, as if I had been one of her sons.

She was very small and very round, but from her pictures I could tell she had been beautiful. She gave off a sweet air of femininity as she pranced about the room and ran back and forth from the kitchen, fixing dinner and talking. We had fried chicken, and she served me three helpings.

"You need to get your strength back," she kept saying.

I asked her where Big Johnny White was. She didn't know. He had stayed asleep till noon, his face to the floor. He didn't remember attacking me.

"Believe you me, I gave him what for," she added indignantly. "That man is worthless—nothin' but trouble!"

There was no telling where he had gone off to. Memphis, Jackson, Tunica. Maybe back to Chicago. It was always like that. He would hang around here and there, a hobo on the highways and railroads, a bluesman wandering all across America.

I tried to tell Lula how much respect I had for Big Johnny's music and how much his music had given to me, that anybody who could have such feeling couldn't be really bad.

She smiled at that, and her glasses slipped down her flat nose. "Ah, if you could only have heard him back then, when he was younger. I was just a kid then."

He had played in all the juke-joints in the area, little

73

shacks for dancing, raised up on stone columns because of all the flooding.

"Children weren't allowed in," she said, "so me and some other kids, we'd crawl in between the ground and the floor and stay there all night listening to the music. They had some mighty fine musicians, but Big Johnny was the best of all. He had such a sweet touch! All the women were in love with him!"

She added, with a mischievous pout, "And he was thin, too. Tall and thin!"

A little later I was standing at the doorway. The bus for Memphis and Chicago was about to leave. Another long night lay ahead of me. "Big Johnny . . . ," I said to her, "if I can arrange for Big Johnny to come to Europe, I'll write you here."

Her face lit up. "Yes, yes, I'll try to find him and somehow we'll get him up on that airplane. He'd love so much to go overseas before he dies."

And her great laughter rang out in the night. The whites of her eyes were shining. I held out my hand to say goodbye, but she grabbed hold of my head with her two hardened hands and brought me to her to give me a wet kiss on each cheek. The way she would have done for one of her sons.

My American trip was coming to an end. I stayed one more day in Chicago, and this time I really was going back to France. I walked everywhere that day and looked for a last time at the places where I had lived, as I suddenly realized now, a unique adventure.

It was a damp, cold day. Not once did the sun break through the thick clouds. Scattered showers soaked the streets and sidewalks. A long line of yellow taxis crept along, on the lookout for a hand emerging from a dripping raincoat to hail them.

Now I was in the Sears Tower elevator, in "the tallest skyscraper in the world," as American advertising put it, which described everything everywhere as "the something-est in the world." But this time it wasn't a lie.

Over five hundred yards up, only a double layer of smoked glass separated a narrow hall from the emptiness outside. The hall was thickly carpeted, with wooden benches and rows of telescopes pointed outward. For a quarter in the slot you could look through them.

But this air-conditioned, heated cockpit was wrapped in cottony fog that beat against the heavy windows.

Hypnotized by all this, I didn't notice the time passing. Night had fallen, and Chicago was plunged into darkness. Suddenly a cold wind blew off the lake, slapping, shoving, hauling away the clouds. Soon the last white whiffs, still clinging to the tower windows, were swept away, and beneath me lay a fascinating landscape: skyscrapers rising in a tropical forest of colored lights and a giant superhighway complex gripping the city, plunging its branches deep into the heart of Illinois and the neighboring states, like a luminous octopus casting its tentacles toward far off prey crouching at the horizons.

On the lake red, yellow and blue lights swung to the whim of the waves and danced the hokey pokey with their own reflections. There were little pleasure boats, big millionaires' yachts, enormous barges loaded with cargo, coming in from or heading out for the rest of the world by way of the Saint Lawrence.

Chicago stretched at my feet. A rug sewn with multicolored stars. A vast megalopolis. A living being filling its steel lungs and here and there exhaling puffs of thick smog.

Here, by the lake, luxuriant reflections in the water betrayed the presence of the rich bourgeois villas, small fortresses with their electric fences and their watch-dogs. Farther off, at the border between the light and the shadows, to the music of a James Brown record, Sugar sat in his pile of junk, recalling days of glory during the War. Even farther, somewhere among those indistinct shadows, some old bluesmen—maybe Big Johnny White, too—were still singing blues songs steeped in the kind of melancholy and squalor that sticks to your skin for a whole life, singing for an audience of poor old men and women, huddled together and remembering Mississippi.

FIVE

As soon as I got off the plane at Orly Airport, from the moment the customs inspector scratched a few angry chalk marks across my suitcase, I knew I was going to have trouble readjusting to France. Something had happened inside me. Some part of Black America had become part of me. I was here, but I was still there. Life started over again, but a strange feeling, insidious, lasting and bitter in my mouth, and a curious rhythm in my blood, kept me from being the same person as before. The ghetto air, the real image of Sugar, undermining the image of my own adolescence, and most of all those days with Big Johnny White, had marked me indelibly. I lived in France and I made a living in France, but my American adventure continued to live inside me. The Chicago nightclubs, the ragged little black children running in the streets, the miserable thugs who robbed me, the nights traveling down through the plains on the Greyhound, Lula's cafe, Big Johnny coming at me with a switchblade—these were the only images of my life I could focus on.

Years rolled by. The weeks in America intensified

and expanded to an eternity. The blues stuck to my skin, not a music but a state of mind, a wretched way of life, an almost satanic art that took possession of me. They were alive and invisible. They prowled around me, omnipresent, goading, crushing. They stuck to me like a film of fog, insinuating themselves into every niche of my life, coming between me and other people, other things. I dragged them around stuck to the soles of my shoes. I knew they were there, sneering, implacable, moody, droning, oppressive, sinister, indispensable. Only my guitar could exorcise them. I played, and I sang, and they eased up, relaxed their grip on me, became sociable, took over my fingers and made them run, lively and nimble, along the six strings. Sometimes I thought I was losing all contact with reality. I no longer doubted that any talent I had was their talent, that any skill was theirs. They made me get up and pick up my guitar. They whispered in my ear, "Play for us," and if I hesitated, if I pretended to think about something else, they would grow threatening, they would bind a girdle of lugubrious thoughts around my soul. Then they would wheedle, "Play, and we'll leave you in peace." Maybe I was going crazy. Whenever and wherever I took up my guitar and cried out my feelings—alone in my room, in the midst of a little group of friends, or more and more often, in public, for a large or a sparse audience—I saw them there. I would take up my guitar, and I would feel them loosen their vise, at first imperceptibly, then more. A few chords, a few arpeggios, and the blues were in the room, executing, with terrifying and mechanical grace, their diabolic dance.

The world around me seemed insipid, drab, but most of all, false and hypocritical. But France was changing. A group of brash students had thrown some paving stones at the forces of law and order and precipitated a revolution in customs, behavior, and attitudes. But as always in France, the show masked the reality. Liberation, revolution, and anti-imperialism were the slogans. But Americanization, individualism, and immediate material gratification were the realities. The French, who had always been fascinated by America, now without realizing it but with uncontrollable and indiscriminate appetite, embraced all the American values. Leftism was chic, and the ardor for freeing far-off peoples from the yoke of imperialism peppered the conversations of our intellectuals. But the movies were American, the ways of thinking were American, the *lifestyles* were American, and so was the music.

In a way, that was lucky for me. I had traveled the road to America before everyone else. I had dreamed the myth and lived the reality. I knew. Because of that, the music was beginning to help me get by materially.

For a while, though, I continued to depend on other work to get by. I moved from office to office, always in an atmosphere that was morally hazy. Nothing was really changing in the Administration. Generations passed, fashions came and went, the old worm-eaten furniture gave way to office material designed and suited to their functions and to the times. The Administration dressed up in new names and was centralized, computerized, and restructured, but the reality remained. The useless still dominated. The old incompetent supervisors with their big leather portfolios gave way to young incompetent supervisors carrying American attaché cases. Costs spiraled upward. The papers, pencils, erasers, staples, and rubber stamps that had once satisfied the masses of parasitic place-holders were replaced by electronic typewriters, sorting machines, stapling machines, word processors. The computers opened their tape recorder eyes wide in amazement as if to ask why their intelligence, their precision, their memory capacity were needed here, where all that flourished was stupidity, imprecision, and haphazardness. All of France was becoming administrative—or tertiary, as administration was called, supposedly because administration came after production and distribution, but in reality because it was third rate.

I took part in this muddle, as modestly and as inconspicuously as possible. My only excuse was that of carnivores that prey on graceful herbivores: they kill to eat; I administrated.

Outside the administration buildings, French music went to jazz, jazz to rock, and rock to blues. The successors of Georges Brassens and Mouloudji sang in English. American performers flocked to France and drew large crowds. Blues singers had their share too, although a small one. A regular shuttle was established between Chicago, New York, and Mississippi on one side, and London, Paris, Frankfort, and Geneva on the other. I managed to get in on the circuit. I knew the language, the music, the places, the people. I became indispensable, a cogwheel linking the European promoters with the American agents and the musicians themselves. I drew up the contracts, wrote letters, translated when necessary, and accompanied the artists on tour. But blues music, even though it was now recognized, listened to, and appreciated, still enjoyed only modest success compared with the immensely popular rock. Everything about the blues tours—the contacts, the concerts, the festivals—had an unfinished, improvised, shabby, thrown-together-at-the-last-minute air. But if it hadn't been, would it have been the blues?

Often I went to meet the black musicians at the airport and drive them to the hotels. They were mostly poor illiterates who had come straight from their ghettos or from their backwater villages, and they weren't equipped to get along outside their own territory. Here they were out of place and disoriented, sometimes not daring to venture outside their rooms.

I remember in particular one tour where a dozen musicians performed very successfully on the great stages of Europe. With their talent, sincerity, humanity, and stage presence, so characteristic of blues artists, they impressed and amazed their listeners, who went away charmed and moved by a music they had known little about. But after the applause, behind the lowered curtain, out of reach of the microphones, what a job it was to try to maintain a little cohesion in that wild group! But that was my job. I had to calm some down, cheer others up, humor others. I also had to keep up with the constant demand for alcohol and try at the same time to limit its effects, which were sometimes disastrous.

What the public never suspected was the quarrels, sometimes violent, and the terrible moments of depression when the blues artist, for all the tribute he was receiving here in France, reminded himself that deep down he was still just a poor nigger momentarily lifted out of his moral and physical misery to receive some shreds of glory, which lashed him more than they warmed him. The politely enthusiastic bravos of Pleyel Hall, though pale compared to the hoots and banter and cheers of the ghetto, brought home to many a blues singer that he was indeed an artist, and more than one singer couldn't take the shock. I saw John Henry hit by a car as he wandered in alcoholic euphoria across the Place de la Concorde during rush hour. Little Sam and Sunny Man, for instance, squared off with knives over some trifle and had to be taken to the hospital, one with cuts across his face, the other with both hands slashed. Robert Junior, lost in his own blues, alone in the midst of five thousand spectators, walked off and went home, with no apparent regrets for the thousands of dollars he was leaving behind and which he would never earn again for the rest of his life.

Big Johnny White was still on my mind. Everything was ready for him to come to France. He had seemed eager to come. And that day long ago but still very near to me, I had promised Lula I'd bring him. Bring him here! That was the idea I talked up everywhere, and it was probably, deep in my heart, my principal motive for continuing, despite the difficulties and the bad pay, to accompany tours. I guided, chauffered, and stoically put up with the other tours with one goal in mind: to pay my debt to Big Johnny White, because I did in a strange way feel I still owed him for his tremendous talent, and for what he had taught me. I had met almost all the other blues artists by now, listened to them, rubbed shoulders with them. But he was the greatest. I had written articles on him. I had made people aware of him. I had nagged a record company until it had retrieved his first work from the dust where it had shamefully lain; from the old molds, they had cut a new album, and it had sold very well. Blues lovers in France knew his name now and appreciated his music. He could come without any problems. Success was certain.

But, as always, he was unreachable. He didn't have any agent, so I was writing to Lula at her little cafe in Clarksdale. She always answered with her tiny, cramped handwriting and uncertain spelling. She could never tell when he'd show up, though he always did. She would talk to him about my letters. He would be enthusiastic, would see himself already in France, would gather the whole neighborhood in to celebrate, would drink, play the guitar, and sing. Next day, he'd be gone. Once, he almost made it. Everything was arranged. But then he got sick and had to go to the hospital. All the while his legend was growing here in France. The very fact that he was one of the few of his generation not to have set foot on the shores of Europe endowed him with an extraordinary aura.

Often at night or in the wee, small hours of the morning, when I came home, I would take out one of his old 78 records and put it on. Above the crackling sound, his guitar would take flight and his voice echo in my room. For the few moments while the old record turned and the needle wobbled, I would be back in Clarksdale, in Lula's cafe.

Finally my tenacity paid off. Standing behind the airport window, I was actually waiting for the arrival of Big Johnny White. Though the media had ignored it, his coming had caused quite a stir among the few but enthusiastic blues fans. At last they were going to listen to, alive and in person, Big Johnny White! The records were remarkable, but what Big Johnny White were they going to hear?

A few years earlier, in Clarksdale, he had been enormously talented, but that had been over there, in the heart of his world, in the midst of his own people. And he had been old, even then. I knew from Lula that he had been very sick, and it was with knots in my stomach that I waited to see him now.

I searched for his tall form among the flood of passengers passing through customs. Suitcases were opened and shut. People found each other, laughed, shouted, hugged. He still hadn't shown up. I was beginning to get desperate and was cursing him for his everlasting irresponsibility and lack of consideration for others. I could see him walking away from his flight at the last minute or just forgetting to take it as he went off to visit some friend in the heart of Mississippi. But Lula had sent me one last telegram. They had driven him all the way to the Memphis airport and hoisted him onto the TWA for New York. Well? Here everything was ready for him: the hotels were reserved, the concert halls had been engaged for months. This wouldn't be the first time a tour had to be canceled because a blues artist had backed out, but what a disappointment it would be this time for everyone, especially for me.

I was enraged, ready to drop the whole project once and for all, when suddenly he was there. Big Johnny White was walking very slowly, with extreme difficulty. His huge legs were no longer able to support him, and he had to rely on a cane. He knew people were expecting an artist, so he was dressed up in his Sunday best for the occasion. A broad white Stetson hid his face. He was wearing a wide-striped gray suit, which hung crookedly on him, rumpled by the long ride in the plane, and a simple leather bowtie pulled the collar of his pale blue shirt tight. He pushed one foot forward a few inches, buttressed himself on his cane, then, with infinite difficulty, dragged the other foot up to the first. I thought about that morning in Lula's cafe when he had almost ripped my guts out in an alcoholic misunderstanding. Big Johnny White! Here he was at last.

With a few strides I was up to him. "Hello!" I said simply, as I caught onto his arm.

He didn't say a word as I helped him along. He leaned on me as he dug into his coat pocket and pulled out his passport. He handed it proudly to me and said his first words on French soil: "That's my passport," and he pointed to the superb photograph of himself, probably taken at the best photography studio in Clarksdale.

I handed the passport to the agent, who looked at it in astonishment. Name: White. First name: Big Johnny. Place of Birth: Friar's Point (Mississippi). Date of Birth:

unknown, sometime in the 1890's. At the bottom of the page was his signature, a large cross in blue ink.

We soon made it to the hotel, a small hotel, because the promoter weighed every franc, and the artist, despite his reputation, probably wouldn't be attracting enormous crowds. In fact, his coming was more the result of an act of faith, a personal stubbornness, than any commercial consideration. I was paying a debt.

But did he even know me anymore? Did he remember our odyssey from Chicago to Clarksdale? It had been a high point in my life. For him, it was nothing. An ingenuous white stranger had visited him and given him a bottle of whiskey and a trip on the Greyhound. There had been a quarrel in a bar and some business with a knife. Just a moment in his life. Whiskey had been his companion since his youth. It irrigated his veins, forming a sugary liquid that today swelled his legs and prevented him from walking right. Travel was a way of life for this itinerant singer: a ride on a freight train caught on the move, a long walk down a long highway, a driver stopping and offering a ride, and a bus ride paid for by a naive, admiring stranger. His knife fights and fights with other weapons were so numerous there was no way he could have sorted them out with precision. Only the most notable remained in his memory, the ones that had earned him jail terms. Once, at least, he had killed a man in a brawl and spent several years working on a chain gang at Parchman Penitentiary.

Now he was sitting on the bed in his small hotel, played out from his voyage. His luggage amounted to one small, brand new traveling bag and his old guitar. The case was peeling off everywhere. He had taken off his hat, so I could take a good look at his face. God, he had aged. He had already been old, back in Mississippi, but now he really was an old man. All he had left for hair was a few scattered tufts of white. His eyes, which didn't see very well, had thick pouches underneath them, and his face was scored with weariness wrinkles. His gigantic behind was crushing the cheap mattress, and, even with the aid of his red, white, and blue-starred suspenders, his pants barely managed to contain his phenomenal belly.

We talked some. Or rather I talked. He grumbled, muttered, shook his head, and didn't understand too well. He was proud to be in Europe, and he knew that people appreciated his music and his records throughout the world.

I showed him newspaper clippings where his work was discussed and where his concerts were announced. On one of them there was an old photograph of him that Lula had dug up somewhere and sent me. He stared hard at it, and his face creased in a broad smile.

"I'm a superstar," he said with satisfaction.

He wanted me to go get him something to eat and, more important, something to drink. I lied and said there wasn't any whiskey to be found in France.

He wasn't fooled. "Cognac will do fine," he said.

As I was setting out in search of some alcohol and something resembling a hamburger, he stopped me at the door: "I'd like a bumper sticker of the Eiffel Tower."

"The Eiffel Tower?"

"Yeah," he answered, pointing with his thick finger, "for my guitar case."

The tour started very badly. There was a total lack of understanding between Big Johnny White and the promoter, Jean Avakian. But that wasn't surprising. The

Frenchman was a jazz fan who managed to get by at the expense of the American artists he dragged around Europe, keeping his overhead to a minimum. As soon as they arrived, he always had them cut records, under no particular label, which he sold throughout the tour.

Big Johnny didn't go out of his hotel without me. Even if he had wanted to, he would have hardly been able to. He was seriously handicapped by diabetes and he needed constant assistance. Besides, he was lost in Paris. This wasn't Mississippi or the Chicago ghetto. He didn't have any focal point to fasten onto. The eating habits, personal relations, ways of doing things were all strange to him. The everyday life of the French was disquieting, disturbing, and most of all, hilarious. He got into the habit of bursting into laughter whenever something unexpected happened.

"This place is full of crazy people," he would say, laughing and coughing. And he would latch more tightly onto my arm, almost making me lose my balance.

But he didn't lose sight of his own interests. When he arrived at the recording studio which the promoter had rented for a few hours, Big Johnny sat down and tuned his guitar.

"Ready to roll!" the sound-engineer called to him after a moment. Avakian watched Big Johnny intently, calculating the rhythm to set for recording enough songs, in the least amount of time, to make an album. Studio time was expensive.

But Big Johnny didn't budge. With infinite patience and not one word or superfluous gesture, he kept on tuning his guitar.

The promoter plucked up his courage and addressed Big Johnny in execrable American: "One is enregistering now, Big Johnny! It is your turn!"

It was very hot. Big Johnny came to a full stop. His broad, tired face was sweating profusely. Icily, Avakian repeated his demand. No response.

The promoter was beginning to lose his temper and, knowing Big Johnny, I was worried that things would turn out badly. I spoke up: "Big Johnny, you're recording now. You need to play something."

The big blues singer turned to me and growled. "Tell this mis'able sonvabitch, this stinkin' insect, he gotta pay if he wants a record from me. Twenty-five dollars, pay in advance!"

He stuck his hand out, palm up.

Avakian, who hadn't understood a word, turned to me, jumping up and down with rage: "What did he say? What did he say?"

At that moment he seemed to match perfectly the portrait Big Johnny had just painted of him, and I had to smile, despite the tension that was mounting in the studio. I tried to explain the situation to Avakian, which wasn't easy. He was pacing the room, bumping into consoles and microphones, with grand waves of his hands, calling upon me as a witness to his troubles and responsibilities. He was a short, puny little guy, squeezed into a tight pair of expensive jeans that gave him a ridiculous look of phony decadence.

As he got more excited, his designer glasses kept falling down his nose, and he had to keep shoving them back.

"But who does he think I am? Who does he think I am? I can hardly make ends meet. I do all this for the love of music, not for money."

He kept turning to Big Johnny, almost sobbing, begging him to reconsider, then off around the room he would go again, threatening and getting more excited.

The old black man didn't move. After a while, as Avakian's sputtering mixture of French and English slowed down, Big Johnny said to me, "Okay, fine. He pays me, or you take me back to the hotel. I'm tired. I need some rest before the concert tonight."

Avakian grabbed me fiercely: "What? What does he say? What does he want to do?"

"He says you have to pay him, or there won't be any record. He told me to take him back to his hotel."

The promoter's resistance collapsed, and he seemed to get even smaller. In adversity, he looked pathetic, cramped—probably his real self, a second-rate little swindler who had chosen to operate with musicians who were neither wealthy nor well educated: chicanery without much profit, but without much risk of a lawyer on his tail.

He pulled out his checkbook, figured up the bill, made a check out, and handed it to me. It was all correct, twenty-five dollars a song for eight songs, at the approximate equivalent in francs. I handed it to Big Johnny and started explaining how to cash it.

He didn't condescend to look at the paper. "I want dollars," he said, calmly wiping his forehead with a big checkered handkerchief, "with eagles on 'em."

I thought Avakian was going to have a stroke.

The concerts in Paris were only fair. The public listened piously. He had taken part in several festivals for young people in America, where they were beginning to get interested in the blues. In comparison to the Americans, French audiences seemed cold to him.

"They didn't like it, did they?" he asked me the first night. I assured him that they did, and I pointed out the young people trying to get backstage to see him in his dressing room.

He was breathing heavily. His legs were hurting. The

hours of playing alone under the spotlight had been hard on him. His face was drawn and his giant frame had shrunk.

"I'm old," he said. "I came too late. They should have heard me twenty years ago."

Out of his pocket he pulled the bottle of whiskey I had resigned to getting for him.

His dressing room was a little wallpapered cubicle with one armchair and a spigot. Some fans were clustered outside the door. They were young people who loved the blues without understanding the words or their significance, without knowing that blues was not just a kind of music but a way of life. They did sense that something important was going on when Big Johnny was on stage.

"We would like some autographs," they said.

"He's tired, you know—" I began, but they insisted. I asked Big Johnny if he wanted me to let them in.

"Yeah, yeah, sure," he answered. He took a big swig of whiskey. "I'm a superstar," he told me one more time.

I acted as interpreter. The French youths stood around the black American in a circle, admiring and self-conscious in their jackets and sport coats. They were students, workers, technicians whom chance had one day introduced to the blues. They clutched their records and handed them to Big Johnny. One or two of them tried to talk to him, but as soon as they saw his total incomprehension of their schoolbook English, they gave it up and turned to me. Big Johnny was sitting down, wiping his brow and nursing his bottle. He held a pen awkwardly in his hand and worked at writing his name in clumsy capitals, the way someone once had probably taught him. The pen slipped from his hand. He managed to get it back between his thick fingers, more at ease with a guitar, and with painful application he carved pen strokes that kept going awry. Some of the letters were missing from his name.

The fans were barely able to decipher the autographs. I thought I ought to offer a word of explanation. "He doesn't know how to write, you know."

One of them, with his hair tied back and wearing a hound's tooth suit, exclaimed, "What? Really? Why not?"

"Most of the blacks of his generation can't read or write. They didn't go to school."

It was as if paving stones had fallen on their heads. From that moment, they looked upon Big Johnny differently, as if a wall had suddenly been thrown up between them. Pity mixed with surprise, disbelief with admiration. They had probably been expecting to meet a great musician, cultivated, eloquent, engaging, one who read and wrote music, one they could have had a nice conversation with. A black Mozart.

The raw reality stunned them; I could tell they were having trouble integrating it into their own mental universe.

Big Johnny White was sitting in their midst, unaware. He had taken off his tie and unfastened his pants to get comfortable. His fly had come open, exposing his polkadot shorts and the folds of his belly.

A wild discussion broke out among the French. Once they got over their shock, they found common ground in their hatred of Americans, who had forced so much injustice on the poor blacks. Their voices rose. I thought of the last song Big Johnny had sung that evening:

> Uncle Sam needs me. They ain't doin' him right.
> Uncle Sam needs me. They ain't doin' him right.
> Gonna pick up my rifle, gonna go out there and fight.

They were getting excited. He was exhausted. An old American Negro, son of former slaves, a tramp, illiterate, alcoholic. A fantastic musician who had, in his own way, built America, the same America that filled the dreams of this noisy French circle of fans.

"Big Johnny's tired," I told them. "You'll have to leave him now."

I had to help Big Johnny change his clothes. It took me a long time getting him to the bathroom, where he let go his overload of whiskey in a long, noisy jet.

As we left the building, dawn was just sticking its nose up, casting a sea-green light on the deserted street. On the sidewalk, the young people were still at their discussion. Some of them saw us and gave us a friendly wave. Others were still lambasting the United States and deploring the fate of the blacks there. A few yards off, a tall Negro, just off the boat from Africa maybe, was shivering over a broom that he was using, awkwardly, to sweep the gutter with. He wore a red wool cap and old, torn gloves to protect his hands. His feet in the water, he came on, methodically sweeping off the curb. When he got up to where the young people were talking, not one of them paid him any attention.

After a few concerts in Paris, we left for more engagements in the provinces. Relations between Avakian and the crotchety blues singer had grown so strained that I preferred to drive Big Johnny around in my old crate. Avakian went his own way, carrying his stack of records to sell, and the sound system, and the only times our paths crossed were at the concerts. Big Johnny refused to be separated from his guitar, so I stashed it next to the spare tire. France had ceased to interest Big Johnny White, and he slept most of the time on the road. Despite all my efforts, he consumed almost as much alcohol as the car did gas: at least a bottle a day. It was frightening, but sadly necessary, because without it he foundered in a deep melancholy interrupted by occasional seizures of rage.

"That trash!" he would shout, speaking of Avakian. "One of these days I'm gonna cut me a few holes in his skin!"

"I know! I know!" I answered, remembering again the morning in Clarksdale in Lula's cafe.

The hotels where Avakian stuck us were increasingly squalid, vile flop houses, in bad repair and dirty, where grouchy porters tossed us rusty keys. The faucets leaked, the pipes clanked, the sheets had suspicious stains on them.

Big Johnny wasn't disturbed. The decor was the kind he had known all his life. You could tell he enjoyed the luxury of just being able to stretch out on a bed every night.

One night, in a little town in the East of France, when I was already in bed, I heard his heavy, faltering footsteps in the creaking corridor. He knocked at the door. I opened, in my pajamas. There he was. Usually he was asleep by this time, or drinking his whiskey, sometimes both at the same time.

"What's the matter?" I asked as I let him in.

He came slowly into the room and sank into the one flimsy chair, dragging under his enormous rear end about half the clothes I had imprudently laid on the arm of the chair for the night.

He didn't say anything, and his eyes shone with a strange light. For the first time since I had known him, he seemed embarrassed.

Gently, I asked again, "What do you want, Big Johnny?"

His hands were folded on his stomach. Hesitatingly,

he let me in on his problem: "My boy," and he took his time before continuing, "you know I'm an old guy, but, you know. . . ."

I noticed he was remarkably well dressed for the time and circumstances. He had on his best shirt and pants, which I had just brought back from the laundry. He had wetted down the few white hairs he had left, and under the room's unshaded lightbulb, they shone from the Brilliantine he had smeared on.

"Yeah, well, I'm old . . . ," he repeated.

There was an interminable silence. I was getting impatient: "Listen, Big Johnny! I'm tired, it's late. If you need anything, just tell me."

"It's, well, you know, usually I don't need any help from anybody else, but here I don't know nobody. I don't talk their talk."

At last he came to the point. "I need a woman, my boy," he said, obviously satisfied with himself for having gotten the request out.

I looked at him in astonishment. He made himself more specific: "I'd like a fat one: they got their sex perched higher on their bellies."

It was eleven o'clock at night in a provincial sub-prefecture of fifty thousand inhabitants. The next day he was giving his only concert at the Youth Center and Center for Local Culture. We were in a fourth class hotel, sore from a chaotic trip in an old 4 L that didn't have a hint of shock absorbers left, and this huge black barrel from the deepest depths of Mississippi wanted me to find him a woman. And not just any woman, a *fat* woman! I tried to reason with him, but he needed a woman the way he needed whiskey, and he couldn't put it off.

"I'm an old man," he said again. "I'm lonely here. I need a woman warm against me."

The half pity, half tenderness, I had been feeling

more and more for this capricious old fat man invaded me again.

"I'll try to find you a woman," I murmured.

It took several calls to the porter to get the address of the only *bar louche* in the area. When I got there I had to shell out several hundred-franc bills to persuade one of the creatures to follow me back to our moth-eaten hotel.

"Why doesn't your friend come himself?" she asked, a brunette in a red dress, the least scrawny of the three bored-looking girls I found there, sipping on drinks they never seemed to finish.

When I explained that he was huge, old, sick, and black, I had to pay double, but at last she followed me to Big Johnny's room.

He was sitting on his bed, dressed in his Sunday best, holding his everlasting bottle. His broad face lit up. "Thanks, my boy, thanks."

A long while later, when I had finally gotten to sleep, there came another knock at the door. I woke up in a rage, leaped out of bed, shoved my shoes half on, and tore open the door.

"What now?"

"Good night, my boy," he said to me, and started back toward his room.

Dumbfounded, I watched his mammoth figure moving down the hall. After a few steps, maybe sensing that I was still standing at my door, he looked back.

"White women," he said, "they're fine, but they smell a little bland."

The first youth center Big Johnny played in had impressed him. "It's nice here," he'd said. "It's like the Greyhound station in Jackson."

This one was just like the other centers where big Johnny had played, except that on the front of the building they had added, "and Center for Culture," because anything was culture in this part of France and the sign looked good and hadn't cost much. The prefabricated plastic structure was a poor province's response to the pompous concrete buildings of the official culture. Its library was stuck in a tiny corner: a few paperback "classics," unread and unopened, and shelves of detective novels, all dog-eared, floppy, and soiled. Next to the library was a wooden cafeteria stand, with names and patterns carved all over its surface with penknives. There was an arrangement of old, torn vinyl couches. Some unemployed kids hung out there, abusing the Foosball table, disassembling their motorcycles, and talking about soccer. The youth director, a castoff from the French academic system, had a luxuriant beard and long hair stuck down the neck of a loose fitting, moth-eaten sweater. He believed in "cultivating" his kids, tore down and rebuilt engines with them, chased their ping-pong balls for them, swept the hall, and tried to hunt up a few not-too-expensive performers to justify his grant and his salary. The blues were a natural for this. The squalor gave the place a family resemblance to what the blues came from. And thus it was that, sandwiched between a folklore troupe of pale, gaunt Chilenos and an exposition on "Armaments and the Third World," Big Johnny White brought the blues to the concrete boondocks.

This evening, as often happened, the hall was nearly empty. Some twenty people had braved the autumn rain to come sit in plastic seats and listen to Big Johnny sing. I was getting worried about his health. Our hard traveling was obviously wearing him out, and his music was getting rougher. He always took pleasure in performing, and often I had to signal to him that he had more than fulfilled his contract and should stop, but his fingers were becoming hesitant and almost day by day his voice was getting weaker. Sometimes he would get choked in the middle of a song and have to stop to cough, spit into one of his gigantic checkered hand-kerchiefs, and catch his breath.

That evening, for the first time, he asked me to ac-company him. I had played some chords with him in our hotel room, and a few walking bass accompani-ments, just to help him practice. Never in public. I was flattered at first. It was a special honor, because all dur-ing his long career he had been extremely particular about his accompaniment.

But when I saw the drawn look on his face, the pale yellow around his pupils, and the difficulty he had in walking, I understood that he was mainly asking me to keep time during the song.

Before we stepped up onto the little stage, he whis-pered to me, "Son," (it was the first time he had called me that) "follow me carefully. I need you tonight. I feel real old. My fingers feel heavy as my legs."

I had to lead him all the way to his chair, step by step, slowly and carefully.

He settled heavily into the chair, clutching his gui-tar to his enormous stomach, sweating, breathing short. His fingering, which had once been so agile, was stiff. His voice, once warm and overpowering, was hoarse and faint. He got his songs mixed up, made mistakes in his solos, and hesitated too long between notes.

He needed me. I had played with him so many times when he was only a stack of records that I knew his repertoire by heart, phrase by phrase, note by note, mea-sure by measure. I threw all my concentration into my guitar. I tried to follow him step by step, to interweave my notes with his: a lagging behind and a syncopation and there!—we were in sync. He would stumble over an E, and I would relieve him with an A. He would get stuck on a trill and, bending a note, I would pull him out of it. He was having trouble barring; throwing everything I had learned from him into my fingers, chord after chord, I gave him back his sound.

He gave me a look where I thought I read all the gratitude in the world. My eyes welled up, but I didn't have to see to play with him. He needed me, and I had answered his call for help.

Then, all of a sudden, he was no longer an old man shriveled in his own fat. There was a flashing note. He slid the metal tube straight to the guts of the guitar, an angry chord, and once again he was superb. His song became bitter and passionate, and his thick fingers caressed his guitar with a delicate tenderness. His flabby body became taut from the tension within it.

He was king again, immense, imperial, magnificent. In that makeshift plastic and plywood hall in the East of France, before a few dozen spellbound spectators, he was what they had been waiting for: Big Johnny White, the greatest of the blues musicians.

SIX

For more than three weeks the cultural centers had given way to theater halls; the youth centers to old, unused movie houses, as we made our curious tour of France, chugging along the autumn roads in a 4 L that was threatening to give up the ghost. But the car wasn't the only one needing rest. Big Johnny was close to a physical breakdown. Even I was having trouble holding up. To keep his costs down, Avakian was imposing a frantic rhythm on us, with long miles between stops and little rest. We often played till three in the morning and were on the road by eight to get to our next town in time to try out the sound system, which also was wearing out, and get a couple of hours' sleep and a light snack. I had to keep constant watch over Big Johnny, get him up to his room, bring him a little to eat and lots to drink, rouse him out of the lethargy that was becoming his normal condition, and get him to the concert on time.

A dull fatigue was taking control of me. A hammering in my head kept me from sleeping. But my body was still young, and I had reserves to draw on. Big

Johnny's reserves had long since been depleted, some-where between Chicago and Clarksdale, maybe at Parchman Penitentiary. Only some miracle kept him going. Every night, the performance was a crucifixion. Only my presence, my guitar, made it possible for him to play so many hours. Sometimes, starting to go on, he would falter, wiping off the rivulets of sweat (despite the gradually cooler weather) and lean on me, almost crushing me, as we walked on stage together. He was an old man getting weaker and weaker, a distant mem-ory of what he had once been, a ghost of the blues.

Near the town of Orange, in Southern France, he broke down.

A few hours before the concert, I found him hunkered over the bidet, vomiting a vile mixture of blood, whis-key, and food. With great difficulty, I helped him stand up, and got him over to his bed. He collapsed with a loud sigh.

"I don't feel good," he said.

I ran to call a doctor and notify Avakian, who was still staying out of our way. They were both there within a few minutes. The doctor took Big Johnny's pulse. I could tell he was concerned.

"I think it would be best to put him in the hospital," he told us.

This threw Avakian into another fit. He cursed at me, accusing me of getting his musician sick. He cursed at Johnny, who little by little was getting his breath back.

"So!" he screamed, waving his hands wildly in front of the shocked doctor: "Big Johnny White! What a fine idea this was, to bring an old drunk here, a human dere-lict! What about me? How am I going to make up my losses if you cancel the concert? I don't have any salary, you know. Hell, I'm doing this for the love of music, to give the public a chance to hear a few legendary artists! I'll sue you both!" He shook his finger in my face. "You're under certain obligations, you know."

The voice of Big Johnny White filled the room, forcing Avakian to keep quiet and try to understand the English. "I'll play tonight," Big Johnny said, directly to me, "and every night until we finish the contract."

I translated for Avakian, who quickly calmed down. "Yeah, yeah," he said. "Fine, then. A pill or a shot, huh Doctor? He'll be all better. Nothing serious." And he left us, grumbling about the sound system.

The doctor must have been wondering what kind of bad play he had landed himself a part in. He held his satchel, rocking back and forth on his heels, as if trying to decide what to do next.

Big Johnny beckoned me over. "Son," he said, "pass me the whiskey bottle. It's there in my travel bag."

When he saw me open the bag and take out the bottle, the poor doctor thought he had to intervene. He pushed me back with his hand: "No, no! Not that! That would be suicide!"

With enormous effort, Big Johnny sat up on his bed. "How old are you, Doc?" he asked.

I translated. Nonplussed, the doctor stammered, "Forty-two, why?"

"Forty-two," I said to Big Johnny in English.

The old man found enough strength to laugh. "I'm maybe twice as old as you, Doc! I've drunk at least one of them bottles a day since my mamma weaned me."

In hardly more than the time it took me to translate this, Big Johnny had finished off another one. "You think you gonna manage to live long as me?"

We gave a good concert, surprisingly good considering everything. As he began one of his songs, Big Johnny looked over to me with a conspiratorial grin:

I'm an alcoholic, yeah, and I regret it.
I'm an alcoholic, yeah, and I regret it.
*'Specially when the liquor store man won't give me no
    credit.*

In Orange, as in other towns, fans gathered at Big Johnny's dressing room, pressing him with the same naive questions, asking for autographs or advice about playing some guitar chord, or just standing there looking at him, until he was exhausted and I had to shoo them off.

That night a middle-aged man with salt-and-pepper hair came up to me and held out his hand: "Don't you recognize me?"

It took me a moment to locate his picture in one of the pigeon holes of my memory. "Claude! What are you doing here?"

He had been my roommate when I was at the university. We hadn't been close friends, but I liked him. He had graduated in English and had gone off to teach somewhere in Normandy. We had corresponded for a while, then time had done its work and we had lost touch.

He seemed delighted to see me again: "I'm teaching in the high school here. For ten years, now. I finally got back down South again!"

I remembered that he had been terrified at the thought of moving farther away, and his ambition from the first had been to get back to Southern France as soon as possible.

"You're guitar playing's gotten good," he said.

He turned and started talking to Big Johnny, in an almost perfect English Big Johnny didn't understand a word of.

Out of habit, I translated, then realized that Claude was hurt. I quickly reassured him. "Big Johnny's English doesn't have anything to do with Oxford English, or even Harvard English."

For a little while we stood talking about the old days and the different roads we had traveled since. He directed a cinema club in Orange and was on the board of directors for the youth center. "That's how I got to sign Big Johnny up to come here. Don't think I've forgotten those old records you were always playing! I guess I must have caught the American virus from you. I do a rather good job on the guitar and the banjo. I play social-activist folk songs."

I glanced at Big Johnny, who was sitting on a little formica chair. He was breathing heavily, clearing his throat, and wiping his brow with his handkerchief.

"We're going to have to go back to the hotel," I told Claude.

When he heard the name of our shabby hotel, he flared up. "You can't stay there. Come stay with us. I have a big house, and I want to introduce you to Magali."

He took each of us by an arm. Big Johnny wheezed and didn't understand a word.

"I guess not," I said, "but we're playing in Nimes tomorrow night. That's not far from here. We could come by and have lunch with you before we leave."

Even though Orange wasn't a very big town, I had trouble finding his house. We got there barely in time for aperitifs, with our bags and guitars stuffed in the back of the 4 L.

Magali was charming. So were their two tall children, a beautiful girl and a lively teenage boy. Already! Hadn't it been just yesterday that we were learning English together in Paris? What with America and France, office work and the guitar, the blues and the blacks, I hadn't noticed the time passing. Claude had his high school, where he taught only thirteen hours a week, his wife, his children and his house. And he was obviously happy. I was traveling from flop-house to crummy hotel, transporting an old, almost crippled alcoholic in a car with its engine shot and a body that showed its years in rust, for a little pay that a sleazy promoter would probably try to argue me out of.

Claude took an obvious pleasure in making us welcome. He filled our glasses with whiskey and tried to talk with Big Johnny, but when he received no response at all he didn't insist. Magali was an excellent cook. The meal was delicious, full of the aromas of the herbs and spices of Southern France. We hadn't eaten that well since the beginning of the tour.

"All the vegetables come from our garden," she told us proudly when I complimented her.

Big Johnny had picked at his ratatouille, chewed on a little meat, and finished off the whiskey bottle. His size and his gaping fly, revealing his polkadot shorts, had obviously surprised our hosts. Now the bluesman sprawled asleep in a lawnchair, his mouth half open, snoring lightly.

Magali questioned me some about Big Johnny and didn't hide her astonishment at the state he was in. Before I could make any response, Claude pontificated, "Those racist American pigs! There's how they treat black people."

Then they spoke to me about their political activities. From Orange they supported distant causes that let them get carried away, to vibrate, to suffer, to struggle, to hope . . . in short, to live. Viet Nam, Algeria, Cuba. Ah, Cuba! Magali was a professor of Spanish, and she was inexhaustible on the subject of Cuba. She and Claude had gone there on a trip sponsored by the Ministry of Tourism and Work:

"They are building a better world directly under the threat of North American guns."

We didn't know the same America. For them, despite the literature, music, and movies, all of which they adored, America remained frightful, crass, imperialist . . . the Antichrist. For me it was Sugar and Big Johnny, the Greyhound bus, the music, the comicbook heroes, the ghetto and the wealth, the freedom to come and go, to live and to die, too, a land of contrasts, sure, neither good nor bad in itself; a society with plenty of faults, but open and mobile, and finally an absolutely fascinating country. I loved it.

I tried for a moment to make them see all this, but they weren't listening. With sweeping gestures they called upon Big Johnny's imposing carcass where it overflowed its chair, sunk deep in sleep, as material evidence: "Oh, yeah, it's beautiful, your America!"

I reminded them, when I could get a word in, of the camp for French Arabs, former soldiers in the French army from Algeria and their families. We had accidentally stumbled on the camp a little earlier while looking for the two teachers' house. It was a dirt road through some prefabricated houses that didn't have running water and were crammed with families, including those ragged, curly-haired, smiling kids who had shown us the way back to the right road, the road for real whites, not their road. But I was wasting my time. Only the abominations of America interested them.

I changed the subject. We had some coffee, and Claude, self-conscious to be playing in front of a "specialist," as I had become for him, interpreted one of Leadbelly's blues songs for me, abusing his guitar and howling frightfully. I complimented him, and he plucked up his courage and played several pacifist folk songs. His D string was at least a half step too low, but he wasn't paying much attention to that as he whacked his guitar, caterwauling and jerking his jaw like Bob Dylan. Magali, as she cleared the table, smiled at us and looked at him with Joan Baez eyes.

We needed to leave, but Big Johnny was resting so comfortably that I accepted their offer to show me around their home and gardens. Magali and Claude made themselves busy opening and shutting the doors of their large house, conducted me to the tool shed, and showed me the greenhouse, where they grew vegetables all year long. The olive grove was vast and beautiful.

"I press my own oil," Claude announced proudly.

At the large garage, we were greeted by two cars, side by side.

"The children are getting older. We're isolated out here," Magali said. "We'll be needing a third car next year."

After I managed to roust Big Johnny out of his sleep and stuff him into the old 4 L, Claude and Magali gave us a bag of olives "for the trip." Then they stood on their little wall and waved to us as I managed to get the car started.

The unpaved road from their house made a straight, dusty line until it joined the road to Nimes. For a long time I could see them in the rearview mirror, still waving.

Montpelier, back east again to Arles, southwest again to Sète, and southwest to Narbonne. Big Johnny's last performances in France were terribly difficult. I had to call another doctor. And then another. Each time it was the same: "We need to make tests. We need to hospitalize him." And each time it looked as if Big Johnny would never make it out of bed, but then a couple of pills and a bottle of whiskey and he was on his feet again. I didn't bother keeping Avakian informed anymore.

It was becoming clear that all the whiskey in France couldn't mend Big Johnny. In Narbonne, in the middle of a song, he had a fit of coughing that wouldn't stop, and I had to lead him off to his dressing room until he could get his strength back. The small audience was fascinated to see a real black bluesman from Mississippi kicking off on stage—you don't see that every day in the provincial capital of Aude. The metal tube, alone and abandoned on Big Johnny's chair, glinted like silver. I picked it up, slipped it onto the little finger of my left hand, and caressed the strings as gently as I could. I played for what seemed like a long time, thinking about Big Johnny White stretched out in the dressing room, trying to get his breath back with big gulps of whiskey. I had given up expecting him when somehow he came back to finish the concert, walking across the stage in infinitely slow motion, one foot cautiously dragged in front of another, as the boards sagged under his weight.

"I don't feel very good tonight," he said to the wildly applauding audience.

This time, in contrast to his usual way, he waited for the applause to die down before starting to play. Then, with his lips almost kissing the microphone, he whispered, "Sometimes you gotta think about God."

And he struck up an old spiritual. He was having trouble singing. I could feel his great body, in its gigantic effort, forcing out a weak and unsteady voice. His fingers fumbled at the neck of the guitar. He was so deep in his hymn, he was concentrating so hard, that the hall was stunned and captive. Suddenly he was no longer playing the guitar. I hesitated a second, then I stopped accompanying.

He finished *a capella*, alone with his microphone, alone with his rhythm, alone with his soul. The audience was on its feet, applauding and calling his name. Big Johnny was a superstar.

As I led him back to the dressing room, I handed back the metal tube I had borrowed.

"Keep it, son," he murmured.

I still held it out to him in the palm of my hand, and he gripped my wrist and closed my fingers around the piece of steel.

"Just now," he said, "when I was in my dressing room, I listened to you playing, and I thought I was hearing one of my old records."

Perpignan was our last stop. The concert had to be cut short, so it was before a somewhat unhappy audience that Big Johnny White's French tour ended. As I had expected, we had to fight with Avakian to wrest our pay from him, but he finally let go of our money: a check for me and cash for the musician.

Big Johnny counted and recounted his dollars. He was satisfied.

"I'm rich, son, I'm rich," he repeated several times as the old 4 L sputtered northward over the foothills of the Cévenne Mountains.

Autumn was ending beautifully. The sun struck the forests we drove through. Russets, maroons and browns lining the roads seemed to be cheering for us.

Big Johnny coughed and hacked and coughed, swigged whiskey, and sweated profusely. He fell asleep about four in the afternoon, his head flopping back. It was dark when we reached Mende, three hundred miles southeast of Paris. I was hungry, but he wasn't moving. He seemed to be in a deep sleep.

I hated to leave him alone in the car, so I tried to wake him. "Big Johnny!" I shook him. He didn't budge.

I realized that he was really sick this time: it wasn't just the whiskey.

I got him into a hospital. After a few hours' wait, I was asked, "Are you one of his relatives?"

I got tangled up in obscure social security transactions, but at last, after I had produced his improbable passport and presented it to the hospital administrators, a wide-eyed orderly deciphered it, and I was able to get some sleep.

Big Johnny stayed ten days in the hospital. I got a room in Mende and went to see him during visiting hours, morning and evening. He had tubes stuck into him everywhere, in his nose and in the veins of his wrists, where there flowed, drop by drop, a sap that was not whiskey. He was getting thin.

At night I would walk the deserted streets of the little town, passing and repassing the stern cathedral. A frozen wind was blowing in from the mountains, maybe warning of snow.

At the hospital, when they realized the old black man occupying a bed in room 43 didn't have anyone but me, a doctor came and talked to me: "Your friend won't make it you know. He's gone into an alcoholic coma too deep to come out of. Will you be staying here till the end?"

The thought of abandoning Big Johnny hadn't come into my mind. I said yes.

He didn't regain consciousness. His complexion turned gray, his skin got flabbier. He had been born somewhere in Mississippi, a little before the dawn of the twentieth century, the son of former slaves. His destiny had been to amuse and to move his neighbors, his friends, his people. In the end, the wish he had shared in that cafe in Chicago had come true: he had traveled across France and had shone, in a way, like the superstar he had dreamed of being.

He might have died in a brawl. He might have been lynched. He might have left his skin in the horrible Parchman Penitentiary or on any of the roads he had traveled. He died on November twenty-fourth in the hospital at Mende, the principal city of Lozère.

"Whom should we notify?" they asked me. In response, I suppose, to the perplexed look that met them, they added, "Where is he to be buried?"

I decided to telegraph Lula. I put together all the money Big Johnny and I had received from Avakian. It was enough to pay for a simple casket, transportation back to Clarksdale, and a small tombstone. I left it for Lula to decide on the appropriate words and have them inscribed.

I went to Orly to see the plane off. As it rose and grew smaller in the distance, I waved goodbye. When I got back to my car, there, wedged into the right front seat, his old guitar waited.

I moped around Paris for a while. Nothing much appealed to me anymore. I had to think about going back to work, because almost all my pay had gone for burial expenses. I didn't know if I should start up another tour, with some jazz or rock group, or get an office job again.

One morning, with no thought of where I was heading, I got into my car and left Paris as a cold winter sun was slowly dissipating the fog. I drove, almost letting the steering wheel turn itself, taking the back roads, until I found myself far to the northwest of the capital. As I enjoyed a steaming cup of coffee in a dank little cafe, I was overwhelmed with an urge to see the English Channel of my childhood again, to smell the salt in the wind, to hear the seagulls, smell the fish being brought in.

I arrived mid-afternoon. I made a tour of my memories, creeping along in the 4 L. The port now was completely reconstructed. The American base had been dismantled. The prefabricated school building of my childhood had been demolished, and in its place a new building welcomed pupils of both sexes, in faded jeans and shirt tails flapping out, laughing and talking, their Walkmans on their ears.

There was no more rubble. There were no more ruins to wander around in. There were no more cranes. There was very little stirring.

The Brasserie du Port was still there. The pinball machine had changed, but the tables Sugar and I had leaned our elbows on had not. I ordered a drink.

The room was three-fourths empty. Some retired people were playing cards. Two young people were having a conversation. As far as I could see, the pretty *filles de joie* had all vanished. The Americans had gone home, and their hostesses turned back into conventional people again.

A nice round grandmother with white hair and a checked apron brought me my drink.

"Is Thérèse still here?" I risked asking her.

She looked at me in astonishment out of green eyes nesting in wrinkles, her skin tanned by wind and time, and I realized my blunder.

"I am Thérèse," she said.

My father was no doubt still alive. After I moved to Paris I had written him regularly, but he had answered only rarely. For a few years, from time to time, I'd get a letter in tight, stingy handwriting. Then, nothing. I kept writing for a while, but, lost in my American dream, bogged down in the blues, I also stopped writing. The thread of communication between us, which was never more than tenuous, broke. But the deeper thread, the color of blood, couldn't.

My family home no longer existed. It had been replaced by a five-storey apartment building. Almost the whole neighborhood had changed in the same way. The craftsmen and shopkeepers had been replaced by renters and investors. Only the butcher had survived. Walled around by concrete, growing old in his cold room, he still worked his knife and cutting block. I asked him about my father.

"The old clockmaker? He lives up on the hill now. He still comes to see me once in a while."

It was past seven, and he was in a hurry to close up shop. He put away slabs of meat and utensils as we talked and he told me the address where I could find my father.

"He's all alone," he said. "You one of his sons? That will make him so happy, to have a visit from you."

Suddenly I wanted terribly to hold my father in my arms before he was pierced with tubes and had to give up his soul, surrounded by anonymous and hurried white uniforms.

I rang the doorbell. A pause, some footsteps, then an eye behind the barely opened door.

"Who is it?" I recognize his voice—more quavery, more hesitant, but his voice, the one that used to tell me over and over, "Clock repair is a clean trade."

I told him who I was, and he let me in.

"I'm glad to see you again," he said.

Furniture from long ago seemed to devour the little space in the apartment. We talked a little. He couldn't hear well. Then I realized that he didn't know clearly who I was; he got me confused with my brothers and asked about my sister-in-law as if she were my wife.

"You have beautiful children," he said.

He insisted on serving me a little liqueur. He poured the sweet alcohol into the little glass, with difficulty, but with the same attention to small actions that I had always known.

With his lens lodged in his eye socket, for years and

years he had scrutinized the guts of time until his eye had let him down, his hand trembled, and his back hurt him too much, from always bending over.

Old clockmaker, what did you see in those cogs and springs? What creature, locked behind those dials, was so precious that you never gave me a look? What gold or platinum screw, what philosopher's stone of precision were you looking for so methodically that you never let go of your tweezers to hold my hand? Who were you really, old clockmaker?

I decided to head back that night. But along the cliff road over the Channel, I stopped. The sky was clear, the stars were shining, but fog was beginning to rise from the blackish waters. The waves beat on the rocks below, slosh and suck, slosh and suck. A little farther off, a lighthouse beacon was sending its crude white light out to the boats, dancing a saraband of little points of light on the horizon.

I stood for a moment watching this, fascinated with the lights and night. Sugar, Big Johnny, old clockmaker father!

An immense wave of emotion washed over me. As I was getting back into the car, I noticed again the form of Big Johnny White's old guitar.

Almost mechanically, I pulled it out and took it from the worn case bearing the magnificent Eiffel Tower bumper sticker I had gotten him. The strings sounded horribly out of tune. My fingers were stiff from the cold and the wind, and tuning took a long time.

The English Channel moon was overhead, with a glaucous halo.

One song followed another. Despite the cold and a north wind that lashed my face and hands, I could feel the instinct and skill returning to my fingers. The lighthouse swung its spotlight and the waves beat time. I improvised a long blues song in A minor, the saddest and most homesick key there is.

From time to time, I heard the clack of heels on the road. The footsteps would stop, probably out of surprise at the musician serenading the sea, then would continue and fade into the distance.

I was facing the water, and the cold was beginning to get to me. Suddenly I had the impression someone was watching, and I turned my head.

A boy was standing a few feet from me. He was fourteen or fifteen years old, with curly hair. He looked North-African. He was carrying some dirty baskets with holes in them and wearing mud-stained sweat pants and a huge pea jacket that almost swallowed him, with wide pockets for his hands to keep warm in. The lighthouse beam struck his face, and I caught the unmistakable look of wonder as he listened to my long blues.

I gave him a little smile, which he responded to immediately. His white and crooked teeth flashed in the night.

"You play awful good," he said.